Science
BEYOND THE
CLASSROOM

AN NSTA PRESS
JOURNALS
COLLECTION

Linda Froschauer, editor

Arlington, Virginia

NATIONAL SCIENCE TEACHERS ASSOCIATION

Claire Reinburg, Director
Jennifer Horak, Managing Editor, Books
Judy Cusick, Senior Editor
Andrew Cocke, Associate Editor
Betty Smith, Associate Editor

SCIENCE AND CHILDREN, Monica Zerry, Managing Editor
SCIENCE SCOPE, Kenneth Roberts, Managing Editor

ART AND DESIGN, Will Thomas, Director
    Cover Design, Tracey Shipley
PRINTING AND PRODUCTION, Catherine Lorrain, Director
    Nguyet Tran, Assistant Production Manager
    Jack Parker, Electronic Prepress Technician

NATIONAL SCIENCE TEACHERS ASSOCIATION
Gerald F. Wheeler, Executive Director
David Beacom, Publisher

Library of Congress Cataloging-in-Publication Data
Froschauer, Linda.
  Science beyond the classroom / Linda Froschauer.
     p. cm.
  ISBN-13: 978-1-933531-37-3
  ISBN-10: 1-933531-37-1
 1. Science--Study and teaching (Elementary)--Activity programs. 2. Science--Study and teaching (Middle
school)--Activity programs. 3. Science--Study and teaching--Parent participation. I. Title.
  LB1585.F76 2008
  372.35'044--dc22
                                    2008018494

Science
BEYOND THE
CLASSROOM

Contents

Section 3. Beyond the School Day: Clubs and Expositions

Section 4. The Family: Take-Home Projects and Family Science Events

Section 5. Informal Institutions: Museums, Zoos, and Other Field Trips

Introduction

Extending Science Learning for Elementary Children

This book is for those who are interested in providing, student with science-learning experiences that go beyond the learning that takes place within the usual school day and within the school building. Establishing science clubs, designing family science events, creating opportunities for students to share what they have learned through an exhibition, field trips to local sites, or overnight experiences—all of these and more are explored through looking at possible extensions. This book is designed not only for teachers in the formal setting of a school but also for scout leaders, club sponsors, people teaching their children at home, and any parents who want to take advantage of additional opportunities for their children—anyone interested in extending student science learning will find valuable information within this collection of articles and resources.

The impetus for this compendium came from an understanding of the value of experiences that go beyond what can be offered to students during the school day. The National Science Education Standards stress the importance of incorporating informal learning opportunities such as field trips and special programs into the curriculum, because they provide access to the world beyond the classroom and tap into student interests (NRC 1996). The Standards emphasize that this applies to the entire science program and all students in all grades.

Specific groups of students may be of particular interest in your work. This book will help in seeking out opportunities for these special groups. One of those groups is girls: Gender issues are important when considering science for all. Opportunities for girls to be with other girls in communities and activities in which they can do what they want to do—whether they're "good at it" or not should be provided. "Girls need opportunities to explore things that might lead to strong interests and careers, without the pressure to 'win,'" Gina Shaw says (2003). "Make sure she knows people can be good at any doggone thing." Encourage girls to try nontraditional as well as traditional pursuits—take them fishing, work on the car with them, help them build a soapbox derby car. Girls Inc. and the Girl Scouts of America too offer a wealth of ideas.

Although not the only goal of a quality science education, increasing the number of students who select science, technology, engineering, or mathematics (STEM) as a career is one of the aims of providing engaging science experiences. Definitive research is lacking, but, according to the Carnegie Foundation report (1992), the research that has been done, along with retrospective observations by practicing scientists, suggests that the following elements are important in encouraging students to aim for mathematical and scientific careers. Many talent initiatives try to address these needs:

- Solid preparation from an early age in math and science content
- Experience with hands-on content
- Awareness of the utility of school-based learning in the workplace
- Exposure to role models and mentors who work in these fields
- Access to peers who share these interests
- Learning of content. At some level, knowledge of scientific principles, enhancement of technical or problem solving skills, or other preparation to go on to more advanced work should be expected.
- Enhanced positive attitudes—even excitement—toward the discipline
- Increased self-confidence in one's ability to excel in this field
- Increased knowledge of the value of math and science in the workplace and increased awareness of math and science careers
- Removal of any barriers to possible advancement in math and science that existed prior to the intervention

In addition, researchers have found variables within the family—such as education of parents, careers of parents, support for student interests—and certain affective and personality traits—investigative and theoretical interests, assertiveness, and motivation among them—to be important components of success in these fields. The articles in this collection encourage all of these elements.

This compendium consists of carefully selected articles from the NSTA middle school and elementary school journals *Science Scope* and *Science and Children*. The articles are just a beginning point. You can adapt them to your needs and let them inspire related activities. They provide an overview of information and ideas that can be modified to fit many needs. Many of them provide step-by-step, teacher-tested instructions and guidelines.

The articles are organized into five sections:

- Beyond the Curriculum: Projects and Challenges
- Beyond the School Building Walls: Using Local Sites
- Beyond the School Day: Clubs and Expositions
- The Family: Take-Home Projects and Family Science Events
- Informal Institution: Museums, Zoos, and Other Field Trips

Each begins with an introduction that gives background on using the strategies in the articles and discusses why the strategies are important. In many cases, information on specific research concerning the strategies is also provided. The introductions also describe each article in the section and provide a list of additional useful NSTA journal articles that can be accessed on the NSTA website *(www.nsta.org)*. For a broader view of the general areas discussed, URLs to additional sources are identified. As with all URLs, take care in using them with students because they may change over time.

Linda Froschauer
NSTA Past President, 2006–2007

References

American Association for the Advancement of Science (AAAS). 1993. *Benchmarks for science literacy*. New York: Oxford University Press.

Shaw, Gina. 2003. *Raising strong, confident girls*. WebMD. *www.medicinenet.com/script/main/art.asp?articlekey=56689*

Carnegie Council on Adolescent Development. 1992. *A matter of time: Risk and opportunity in nonschool hours*. Report of the Task Force on Youth Development and Community Programs. ERIC Document Reproduction no. ED355007.

National Research Council (NRC). 1996. *National Science Education Standards*. Washington,DC: National Academies Press.

Section 1

Beyond the Curriculum: Projects and Challenges

Beyond the Curriculum
Projects and Challenges

If we want to consider science for all, then we must seek ways to engage students in interests that go beyond the curriculum. Solving problems, meeting challenges, and working with others on projects can all provide for conceptual understanding by enthusiastic students. But, problem solving and projects take additional time.

The National Science Education Standards and Benchmarks for Science Literacy stress the importance of creating science experiences that are linked to the real world, something that is familiar to students. Projects and challenges hold the potential for fostering curiosity and motivating students.

Most curricula developed for use in public schools take into consideration the time limitations felt by many elementary teachers. We know that challenges and projects take additional time and are frequently omitted from the choices provided to teachers. These are the types of activities, however, that encourage students and engage them in learning: They should not be considered tangential to developing conceptual understanding.

Lillian Katz, professor emerita at the University of Illinois and a specialist in early childhood learning, provides this concerning the place of projects within the curriculum:

Communicative skills develop when there's something meaningful for children to communicate about-when they are taking an active role....

Advocates of the project approach do not suggest that project work should constitute the whole curriculum. Rather, they suggest that it is best seen as complementary to the more formal, systematic parts of the curriculum in the elementary grades, and to the more informal parts of the curriculum for younger children. Project work is not a separate subject, like mathematics; it provides a context for applying mathematical concepts and skills. Nor is project work an "add on" to the basics; it should be treated as integral to all the other work included in the curriculum:

Systematic instruction
1. helps children acquire skills;
2. addresses deficiencies in children's learning;
3. stresses extrinsic motivation; and
4. allows teachers to direct the children's work, use their expertise, and specify the tasks that the children perform.

Project work, in contrast
1. provides children with opportunities to apply skills;

2. addresses children's proficiencies;

3. stresses intrinsic motivation; and

4. encourages children to determine what to work on and accepts them as experts about their needs. Both systematic instruction and project work have an important place in the curriculum.

[Projects] provide lots of opportunities for children's natural curiosity to manifest itself. With very young children, our role is one of supporter and guide. With preschoolers and older children, we need to be more challenging, involve children in projects. I define "project" as an in-depth investigation of a phenomenon or an event in children's own experience or environment that is worth learning about—something children are interested in, something they can readily observe and interact with. During project work, we help children formulate their own research questions, figure out ways to find the answers, and assist them in representing their findings. Worthwhile projects contribute to children's confidence in their own experiences and help them understand those experiences more fully. (1993)

If you are seeking concrete ideas as to how you might structure a project or in-depth inquiry, the Northwest Regional Educational Laboratory (NWREL) provides an excellent guide on its website. It includes step-by-step instructions as well as exemplars.

In This Section (articles are in italics)

This section begins with an article that sets the stage for students to become problem solvers. *Problem Solvers to the Rescue* creates an environment where a simple, realistic problem challenges students to consider a variety of issues and how to overcome them. The model provided through this scenario can be applied to many problems.

There is nothing like being a scientist and sharing real scientific data with other "scientists." In *S'COOL Science* students serve as researchers. Students collect data and share their observations of clouds online with other students conducting the same type of research as well as with NASA researchers. Student observations help NASA scientists calibrate their satellite data.

Design Challenges Are "ELL-ementary" provides insight to the issue of providing quality science experiences for all students, including those with English as a new second language. The design challenges allow students to work in the content area without relying heavily on their English skills. They are allowed to express what they know through their designs rather than language. But, even as language is not the emphasis of the lessons, students develop new vocabulary and use it immediately.

Science and art combine as a way to engage students in subject matter that is high interest in *Every Feather Tells a Story*. Direct observation of the characteristics of feathers comes from a discussion of birds and how their feathers differ from one another. The student's study of form and function lead them to an art lesson in which they create an imaginary bird. This article serves as a model that may be adapted to fulfill the requirements of a curriculum area while extending the conceptual understanding developed by students.

Valuable lessons can be earned through using the local environment while comparing it to the entire country. The Journey North Project inspires students in kindergarten through grade two not only to monitor plants in their own surroundings but also to go online to track the growth and blooming of flowers across the United States. *Tracking Through the Tulips* provides a glimpse into the process from soil analysis and planting tulip bulbs in the fall, inquiring about plants all year, and on to monitoring the growth and blooming progress throughout the spring. It is an example of how the local community can be connected to the entire nation through the World Wide Web.

References

Katz, L. 1993. The project approach presentation paper. ERIC Clearinghouse. *http://lone-eagles.com/courses/rfts/ti2kat.htm*

Katz, L. 2002. *Early childhood today interviews: Lillian G. Katz, PhD, on how children learn through cooperation*. New York: Scholastic.

National Research Council (NRC). 1996. *National Science Education Standards*. Washington, DC: National Academies Press.

American Association for the Advancement (AAAS). 1993. *Benchmarks for science literacy*. New York: Oxford University Press.

Northwest Regional Educational Laboratory (NWREL). 2002. Project-based instruction: Creating excitement for learning. Portland, OR: NWREL. *www.nwrel.org/request/2002aug/implementing.html*

Resources

The articles listed are available through the Learning Center on the NSTA website at *http://learningcenter.nsta.org*.

Lindgren, C. 2006. Send your students to Mars. *Science Scope* 29: 58–61.

Green, S., and J. Smith. 2005. Small things draw big interest. *Science and Children* 42: 30–34.

Sterling, D. C. 2007. Modeling problem-based instruction. *Science and Children* 45: 50–55.

Thomas, J. Cooper, and D. Haukos. 2004. Skateboards or wildlife? Kids decide! *Science and Children*. 41: 20–24.

Tretter, T. 2004. Science in the toilet: The flush of learning. *Science Scope* 27: 30–33.

Problem Solvers to the Rescue

By Frances V. Figarella-García, Lizzette M. Velázquez-Rivera, and Teresita Santiago-Rivera

Imagine … you must bring water to a hurricane-ravaged area. There is only one bridge and only one truck, and the bridge can only hold so much weight. Your calculations determine if the truck—and its load of water—can make it safely over the bridge.

This is a typical challenge during two-week summer camps for third- through fourth-grade students held in the Construct, Discover, and Learn (CDL) schools across Puerto Rico. The camps—and the CDL schools in which they take place—are part of a systemic professional development program directed by the University of Puerto Rico Resource Center and sponsored by the Puerto Rico Department of Education to support the development of inquiry-based science and mathematics instruction for elementary students.

Our school, University of Puerto Rico Laboratory School in San Juan, is a designated CDL center in which summer camps are held. Through the assistance of university faculty, our center has provided more than 120 teachers guidance and support in implementing inquiry-based instruction. This article describes a typical camp session and some of the things we (a university professor and two classroom teachers) have learned from our experience as camp coordinators.

A Problem to Solve

Since our program began in 1999, we have focused on the design of science curriculum units using the constructivist methodology of problem-based learning (PBL). We decided to plan lessons specifically related to the concepts of mass and volume because (1) these concepts are not commonly taught at the elementary level in Puerto Rican schools, even though they are fundamental concepts for this level; and (2) even when these concepts are taught, it is often done in a traditional way—through the use of the textbook, without hands-on activities (Gabel 1994).

Delisle (1997) introduced a specific structure that facilitates the use of PBL, which we adapted to suit our instructional objectives. We followed these steps:

1. Present the problem.
2. Generate possible solutions.
3. Explore what is known using a Know-What-How (KWH) table (Fosnot 1996; Brooks and Brooks 1993).
4. Identify the most convenient method to solve the problem.
5. Conduct activities to learn the concepts needed to solve the problem.
6. Apply new concepts to solve the problem.

7. Present the solution to share and demonstrate the knowledge constructed.

Water Over the Bridge

To present the problem to students, we held a hypothetical public hearing in which two teachers, representing the mayor and a community member of a town in Puerto Rico, dramatized the following scenario:

The community member was seeking help from the mayor because the town was running out of water. A hurricane had damaged a bridge in town that was the only way to get into the community. A provisional yet fragile bridge substituted the original one, but vehicle transportation was restricted.

The mayor was willing to provide a municipal truck to carry the water, but he didn't know if the bridge would support the truck's mass or what volume of water the truck would transport. The mayor needed advice from a scientific team who could determine the mass and water volume the bridge could support. The mayor invited the students to be the scientific team to help solve the community's problem.

The students were excited to accept the challenge. The teachers discussed the situation and asked students to explain the situation in their own words. For the most part students assessed the situation accurately (i.e., "A hurricane passed through Jurutungo. The people have no water and the provisional bridge is falling down. The mayor wants scientists (us) to find the maximum amount of mass that the bridge can hold and the maximum volume of water that the truck can take in just one trip").

However, there were some students who focused on nonessential aspects of the situation, asking such questions as, "How long has the town had the water problem?" and "How do children go to school, if the cars cannot cross the bridge?"

The teachers helped students focus on the part of the situation they could solve and made sure everyone clearly understood all the information provided to them.

We'll Solve It!

Next, students began brainstorming possible solutions. Some of their ideas included carrying water by foot, transporting the water through a very long hose, building a new bridge or a water pipe, and transporting water by helicopter. The teachers asked such questions as, "How far is the bridge from the community?" "How much water can a helicopter transport?" "Does the town's mayor have a helicopter available to transport the water?" "How much would it cost to construct a new bridge?" and "How long would it take to build the bridge?" to help students realize that these were not feasible solutions to the problem.

The teachers reminded students the mayor had already evaluated the municipality situation and the town's available resources and had decided the best (and most immediate) solution was to transport the water by truck in one trip, using the provisional bridge. But to make sure his decision was right, he needed their help as scientists. Their job was only to help him determine the mass and volume that the bridge would support, not to bring water to the community—that was his responsibility.

As students continued brainstorming ideas about how they might measure mass and volume, they realized it would be dangerous to do tests on the provisional bridge. Instead, the teachers suggested testing their ideas using models and showed students a model bridge that had been previously constructed from inexpensive wood, a plastic toy truck, and several small plastic containers of different capacities.

Procedure via Consensus

After brainstorming, students solidified their ideas by completing a KWH table (Figure 1) to consider what they Knew about the situation, What they needed to learn, and How they could learn it. This organizational step helped students clarify their understanding of the problem at hand and anticipate the steps required to solve it.

Students Knew that the provisional bridge was frail, the community was nearly out of water, and the town mayor had offered a truck to transport the water in one trip. Students also knew What they needed to learn—the maximum mass the bridge could support and the maximum volume of water that could be transported in one trip. Students thought about How they could learn this information—by learning how to measure mass and volume.

When they had completed the chart, the teachers divided students into five groups of four students each and asked each group to design a procedure to solve the problem and present it to the whole class. When each group had come up with a procedure, the teacher and students evaluated the procedures presented by each group, and, via consensus, they chose a general procedure for all groups to follow:

1. Gather the necessary materials (truck model, bridge model, graduated cylinder, platform balance, water, small containers of various capacities, two tables, and adhesive tape).
2. Mount the bridge between two desks and tape in position.
3. Using the graduated cylinder, measure a volume of water in the small container.
4. Measure the truck's mass on the platform balance.
5. Measure the mass of the small containers holding the water on the platform balance.
6. Add the mass of the truck and the mass of the small containers when full of water.
7. Repeat the procedure six times (trials), gradually increasing the volume of water carried each time, to find the maximum amount of water to transport across the bridge in one trip.

Practice Makes Perfect

With the procedure in place, the teachers had students conduct five related activities to help students understand mass and volume. The student groups would

- learn how to use the graduated cylinder,
- measure the volume of water in different containers,
- practice using a platform balance,
- find the mass of water in different containers, and
- estimate (and then measure) the mass of a solid and volume of a liquid.

Figure 1.
A KWH table.
A Know-What-How table helps students synthesize the information at hand before solving a problem.

K	W	H
• The bridge is frail. • The community has almost no water. • The town's mayor has a truck available to transport the water in one trip.	• What is the maximum mass of the truck? • What is the maximum volume of water that could be transported?	• How is mass measured? • How is volume measured?

After each activity, the teachers discussed with students what they observed. By the end of the activities, students had begun to formulate operational definitions for *mass* and *volume* and recognize that mass and volume are physical properties that can be used to describe matter.

Will the Bridge Hold?

Once students were comfortable with their knowledge of how to measure mass and volume, students were ready to apply what they learned to the water problem posed earlier.

So, following the procedure agreed upon earlier in the project, each group was given a plastic toy truck, a bridge, and a selection of different containers with which to conduct their six trials.

Before conducting any trials, students mounted the bridge using the provided instructions; decided the initial volume of water they planned to transport; chose the container in which to transport the water (some containers could transport the same volume of water but had different masses); determined the mass of the water in the container and the truck; and predicted how many containers they could fit on the truck. When all the necessary decisions had been made, students conducted the trial.

Initially, some groups were more conservative than others, transporting only 30 mL or 40 mL of water, while other groups began the trial with larger amounts, such as 120 mL of water. Students recorded the results after each trial, gradually adding more mass and volume until they had completed six trials without breaking the bridge. The bridge bowed under the weight in some of the trials, but never failed.

With each trial, students grew more excited. Some students were fearful the bridge would not hold the mass and volume that was being put on it. Others mentioned the bridge was much stronger than they had expected. The mass and volume of the last trial was the group's maximum support that the bridge could hold.

When each group had completed all six trials, students compared data. Students discovered that each group had determined different "maximum" quantities, so they chose to present the results from the group that transported the greatest volume of water to the mayor.

Making the Case

The teachers documented the whole process with photographs, and students concluded the experience by writing summaries of their camp activities—from the initial public hearing to the problem's solution—and creating a book, which they presented to their parents, the "community member," and "mayor."

The presentation began with a restatement of the problem and a summary of the different activities that led to the solution. Then, students presented the maximum volume of water and maximum mass the bridge could support using the highest amounts achieved by a group in the last trial.

The students also shared their concerns related to the velocity of the truck, the mass of the driver, and the type of containers they recommended using. Students recommended the truck go at low speed, the driver be slim (so that he/she would not add much mass), and the containers be the ones with the lowest mass so they could take more water.

Real-Life Learning

Learning was assessed in several ways throughout the experience. Students completed laboratory journals in which they recorded the data acquired in each activity, wrote answers to analytical questions posed by the teachers, and reflected over the days' events and activities. Other assessment measures included various performance tasks, oral presentations, written reports, and a class-created book describing their experience.

Through these measures, we were able to assess students in several areas: scientific vocabulary; written and oral language skills; cooperative skills; creativity; conceptual understanding of mass and volume; reading numeric scales; measurement skills; mathematics skills, such as addition and subtraction; and science-process skills, such as observation, prediction, inference formulation, hypothesis formulation, and experimental design.

We found students were motivated to learn when they were presented with a "real-life" problem to solve. The hands-on experiences afforded by the PBL methodology enabled students to go beyond learning about technical skills and constructing definitions, and promoted a significant understanding of mass and volume concepts. They played, enjoyed, and learned in a stimulating and challenging environment.

Through the summer camp program, each of us (the teachers) truly experienced being a facilitator for students' learning processes. We concluded that the most important function of the science teacher is to orchestrate hands-on and minds-on activities to promote the process of inquiry, the construction of knowledge, and the development of a scientific culture.

When the new semester began shortly after the camp concluded, we encountered a new challenge: incorporating the PBL methodology into some of our existing curricular units, this time without external financial resources, extra time to plan collaboratively with peer teachers, and the support of university faculty. Could it be done? Given our successful experience during the summer, we would definitely give it our best shot!

Frances V. Figarella-García is a science teacher at the University of Puerto Rico Laboratory School; Lizzette M. Velázquez-Rivera is an associate professor in the curriculum and teaching department at the University of Puerto Rico; and Teresita Santiago-Rivera is an English teacher at the University of Puerto Rico Laboratory School, all in San Juan, Puerto Rico.

Resources

Brooks, J., and L. Brooks. 1993. *In search of understanding: The case for constructivism classrooms.* Alexandria, VA.: Association for Supervision and Curriculum.

Delisle, R. 1997. *How to use problem-based learning in the classroom.* Alexandria, VA: Association for Supervision and Curriculum Development.

Fosnot, T. C. 1996. *Constructivism: theory, perspectives, and practice.* New York: Teachers College, Columbia University.

Gabel, D. L. 1994. *Handbook of research on science teaching and learning: A project of the National Science Teachers Association.* New York: Macmillan.

National Research Council (NRC). 1996. *National Science Education Standards.* Washington, DC: National Academy Press.

Polman, J. L. 2000. *Designing project-based science: Connecting learners through guided inquiry.* New York: Teacher College Press.

Savery, J. R., and T. M. Duffy. 1995. Problem-based learning: An instructional model and its constructivist framework. *Educational Technology* 35 5): 31–38.

Torp, L., and S. Sage. 1998. *Problems as possibilities.* Alexandria, VA: Association for Supervision and Curriculum Development.

Connecting to the Standards
This article relates to the following National Science Education Standards (NRC 1996):

Content Standards
Grades K–4
Unifying concepts and processes
• Constancy, change, and measurement
Standard A: Science as Inquiry
• Abilities necessary to do scientific inquiry
• Understanding about scientific inquiry
Standard B: Physical Science
• Properties of objects and materials

S'COOL Science

By Linda Bryson

You're likely familiar with the fact that NASA conducts many high-tech research projects, such as launching satellites to study Earth's climate. However, you may be as surprised as I was to find out that "regular" people on Earth are sometimes needed to confirm or help interpret the images satellites actually send back. For example, satellites can't easily differentiate between cloud cover and snow pack. Observers on the ground—like our students—can supply needed information.

What a perfect opportunity for my fifth-grade class. This year, my students participated in NASA's S'COOL (Students' Cloud Observations On-Line) Project, making cloud observations, reporting them online, exploring weather concepts, and gleaning some of the things involved in authentic scientific research. As you will gather from our experience shared in this article, the project is very adaptable and can be integrated into many subject areas and used throughout the school year at any grade level. As a S'COOL enthusiast, I encourage you to try it with your students.

S'COOL Beginnings

S'COOL is part of a real scientific study of the effect of clouds on Earth's climate. Students from all over the world add to data collected by NASA's Earth-observing satellites. Matching student observations—called *ground truth measurements*—with satellite readings helps NASA verify and calibrate its data.

When the orbital path of an Earth-observing satellite—either *Aqua* or *Terra*—is over your region of the world (about once a day), students record cloud observations. These observations include *cloud level*—high, midlevel, or low; *cloud type*, such as cirrus and stratus; *cloud cover*, such as clear, partly cloudy, or overcast; and *visual opacity*, such as opaque, translucent, or transparent. See Figure 1 for an overview of cloud types. Students may record some optional data, which includes such surface measurements as temperature, barometric pressure, and relative humidity.

I began our involvement by registering at the S'COOL website (see Internet Resources) and obtaining a password and login—a requirement for data submission. The website has everything you could possibly need, including a cloud tutorial and information about satellites. Each satellite's overpass schedule can be downloaded for your area. Students simply check a box to indicate the types of clouds they see, their level, the overall amount of cloud cover, and the visual opacity of the clouds.

Observations can be made as often as you wish. There is no obligation or commitment on your part to report a set number of observations. Once the report form has been completed, you simply submit the data to the website, a process that takes only a few minutes. The data can also be sent by fax or mail directly to NASA Langley Research Center in Hampton, Virginia.

Clouds and Contrails

The topic of weather is not a part of my school's fifth-grade science curriculum, but I integrate

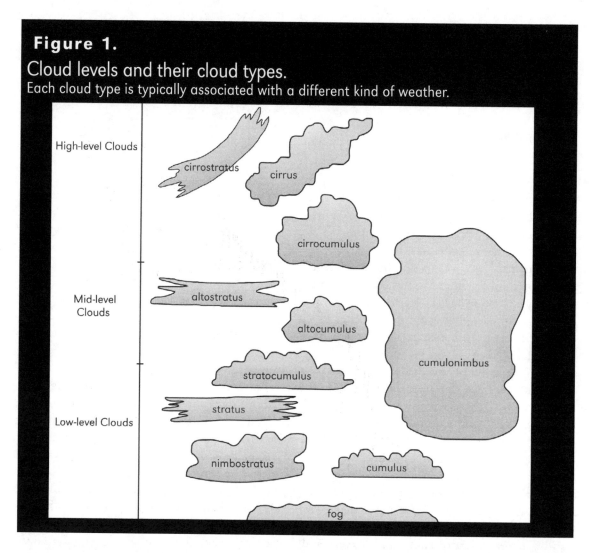

Figure 1.
Cloud levels and their cloud types.
Each cloud type is typically associated with a different kind of weather.

our weather study into reading, social studies, and current events. To prepare students for the project, I started out the school year with a brief introduction to weather; as we talked, I filled in a KWL chart with what we Knew and what we Wanted to learn. At the end of the lesson, I added what we had Learned.

In teaching my students about clouds, I discovered some new things myself, which I shared with the class. For example, *high clouds* hold in solar radiation, and *low clouds* reflect solar radiation, allowing heat to leave Earth's atmosphere.

I also learned about airplane *contrails*—artificial clouds formed by airplane exhaust. During the days following the events of September 11, 2001, when commercial airplanes were not permitted to fly, the actual daily average temperature range in the United States was lower than normal. Scientists are studying this data to see if contrails may be one factor in global warming.

Contrails are also being studied through S'COOL. On the cloud observation report form there are two sections for reporting the number of persistent and/or short-lived contrails present.

With this background in place, students waited with anticipation for the satellite to approach. In the meantime, I prepared three reference sheets of construction paper, writing the words *high, midlevel,* and *low* on them and pasting examples of the different cloud types for that level onto each.

On a wall in my classroom, I hung three different clipboards, one each for the *Terra* and *Aqua* satellite schedules, and one for holding a stack of report forms. As an extra reminder, I wrote the names of each satellite on the chalkboard with the observation times written beside them. A classroom helper (one of the students) was responsible for making sure the observations occurred at the proper time.

Observation Time!

When the time came for one of the satellites to pass over our area, we excitedly headed outside to make our first observation. My students loved going outside to observe the clouds. We made observations together and proceeded slowly as we tried to figure out which clouds were low, middle, or high. It was difficult for the students to identify the cloud types at first, so we discussed what we were observing and filled out the report form together.

As skills improved, rotating groups (of about three students) were sent outside together. This small group had to decide on what cloud type they observed. Once they came to agreement about what to mark down on the report form, they returned to class. On days when there was inclement weather, we completed our observations from inside the classroom by looking out the window.

Students collected data throughout the entire school year. I downloaded and printed our data after it had been submitted and kept it for reference in a colored notebook. Eventually, when the actual satellite data had been reported on the S'COOL website (about two months after submission), we compared our observations to the data the satellite reported and discussed why the information might have differed. For example, we can only see lower clouds on overcast days; while the satellites can distinguish the mid- and higher-level clouds that we can't see from the ground.

Since I have collected data several years in a row, we have previous classes' data notebooks as well. Students enjoyed using these notebooks to compare the cloud cover and temperature information submitted on the same day the previous year.

Ground Observations

My class also participated by collecting the optional surface measurements. Students made ground observations, such as surface cover, temperature, barometric pressure, and relative humidity.

My students learned how to read a thermometer and a barometer, which I purchased from Ward's Natural Science for $56.50 (see Internet Resources). The class also made an instrument to measure relative humidity called a *sling psychrometer* using instructions found on the S'COOL website (see Internet Resources).

To take a reading, students wet the piece of gauze found on one of the two thermometers of the sling psychrometer and swung it around outside for 30 seconds. If the weather was bad, I opened a window and swung the sling psychrometer around outside through the window opening. A chart, also available on the S'COOL website, was used to determine the relative humidity.

Using the equipment gave students valuable experience in making observations and interpreting data: "Now I know how a barometer works. When the barometer number is low, that means there is going to be a storm. If the barometer has a high number, that means the weather is going to be fine. I also learned how to observe weather. When you observe weather, you have to look for what kind of clouds there are and also the temperature and things like that," said one student.

Another student reported, "To find out how warm it is, we use a thermometer. We report it in degrees Celsius (the metric system). I also learned the names of different cloud types like *cumulus* and *stratus*. Also, the lines from the planes that look like clouds are called *contrails*. When we report the humidity, we use the wet-bulb and dry-bulb system."

As a group activity, we also predicted weather based on observing national weather patterns and interpreting weather maps.

Integrated Learning

In November, we read *The Big Storm* (Hiscock 1993). In this story, the path of a huge spring storm is traced across the United States. Hiscock explains what happened each day as different parts of the country encountered this weather system. After reading the book, students wrote "weather reports" and read them aloud to their classmates.

Students also obtained pen pals from a school in Washington state, where "the big storm" originated. The pen pals were also incorporated into social studies lessons. Map skills were reinforced when we practiced locating both schools on a map using latitude and longitude. The distance that separates our two schools was calculated in both kilometers and in miles. We also exchanged local weather maps and forecasts from newspaper clippings with our pen pals.

In mathematics, taking accurate temperature readings had to be introduced or reviewed. Conversions were done between Fahrenheit and Celsius. A lesson on time was also needed, including a discussion of time zones and universal time, the required time for the report form. (I set an alarm clock to remind students when they needed to make an observation.)

In addition to the pass/fail grade students received on the weather report they presented to the class, the class also took a multiple-choice test on *The Big Storm* that came with our reading series.

On a Cloud

All in all, the S'COOL project provided an exciting way to introduce my students to various forms of scientific technology and the excitement of taking part in authentic scientific research. At the end of the school year, my students wrote about what they had learned from taking part in the project.

"I learned NASA has a lot of satellites and how NASA uses the information that schools send in," said one student.

Another student said, "I learned about the *Terra* and the *Aqua* satellites and about different cloud levels like the high, middle, and low clouds." She also suggested an addition to the project: "We should have one wall of the classroom be all about weather—with pictures of different clouds and articles and photographs about weather."

I think I'll include her idea in the next S'COOL year.

Linda Bryson is a fifth-grade teacher at Laurelton-Pardee Intermediate School in Rochester, New York.

Resources

Hiscock, B. 1993. *The Big Storm*. New York: Atheneum.

National Research Council (NRC). 1996. *National Science Education Standards*. Washington, DC: National Academy Press.

Internet

Students' Cloud Observations On-Line
  asd-www.larc.nasa.gov/SCOOL/SCOOL.html
Ward's Natural Science
  www.wardsci.com

Connecting to the Standards
This article relates to the following National Science Education Standards (NRC 1996):

Content Standards
Grades K–12
Unifying Concepts and Processes
• Constancy, change, and measurement
Grades 5–8
Standard D: Earth and Space Science
• Structure of the Earth system
Standard E: Science and Technology
• Understanding about science and technology

Design Challenges Are "ELL-ementary"

By Nancy Yocom de Romero, Pat Slater, and Carolyn DeCristofano

Classmates' excited chatter about a science concept overwhelms a student with trouble processing spoken language. In another classroom, a teacher labors to teach about material properties to English language learners. *"Odio la ciencia!* (I hate science)," mutters one child, who loves the hands-on work but lacks sufficient English to feel successful.

As teachers in a school with large bilingual and special-education populations, we constantly seek new ways to help students access science concepts. And we are not alone. Elementary teachers across the nation are facing similar questions: How do we help our special- needs students and English learners understand challenging, standards-based science content while they are developing English language skills?

Through our work as pilot teachers for the Engineering is Elementary (EiE) program developed by the Museum of Science in Boston (see Internet Resources), we've discovered an exciting answer: carefully conceived design challenges. Design challenges—using science knowledge to design, create, and test some thing or process—encourage the development and use of science concepts and English language in contexts that students find meaningful. In design challenges, students can work with content without relying heavily on language and express their science theories in actions, not just words.

We tested EiE's *Materials Engineering: Designing Walls* unit separately, each in our respective classrooms: a fourth-grade bilingual group studying rocks, minerals, and earth materials, and a second-grade inclusion class studying plants and soil—and had terrific success. We each completed our units in about one and one-half weeks (seven 45-minute class periods). The following is a description of our experiences.

Designing Walls

The unit's design challenge—designing a wall to be built from earth materials that could meet specific criteria—engaged students meaningfully. First introduced in the context of a storybook and later pursued as a real class problem, the unit provided the motivation, thematic focus, and momentum that propelled students through challenging content—new concepts, words, and communication skills. Figure 1 is an overview of the four-lesson unit and how it relates to the EiE curriculum framework.

Before we got started, we gave an overview of engineers and technology with the objective of helping students understand that engineers design technologies—and that technologies

Figure 1.
Engineering unit outline.

Unit Lesson	EiE Design Challenge Framework	Materials Engineering: Designing Walls
1	Storybook introduces a problem that students investigate and for which they design a solution.	Students read *Yi Min's Great Wall.*
2	Activity-based exploration of technology and engineering	Students choose among samples of different materials to perform certain tasks, identifying useful properties.
3	Science exploration of concepts related to design challenge	Students explore and describe properties of different earth materials.
4	Students solve design challenge related to storybook using creativity, science knowledge, and engineering design process.	Students design, create, and test a prototype of a wall (of specified criteria) to protect their school garden.

include any object intended to solve a problem. In small groups, students received mystery objects (identified as technology) hidden in paper bags. Upon opening the bags, students discovered that technology includes items as familiar as toothbrushes, paper cups, and other everyday objects. Students then discussed among themselves where the objects came from and what sorts of problems these objects are intended to solve.

Although this was a simple activity, we were impressed that students picked up on the words and concepts of engineering and technology very quickly. Immediately, they seemed to feel empowered by these additions to their vocabulary. Outside of the lesson context, for example, the second graders would refer to different objects as technology. Instead of sharpening a pencil, a child might be sharpening a piece of technology. The notion that everyday objects were technology had caused students to begin looking at materials in new ways, and we knew we could move onto the rest of the unit with confidence.

Lesson One:
Introducing Literacy and Science Concepts
Before every lesson, we shared science and language objectives with students, raising their consciousness of what we hoped they would gain from the lesson. For example, when the class read about a young girl from China and her efforts to build a garden wall to prevent a marauding bunny from eating her school's garden, we let the students know that we were building their readiness for an upcoming challenge. Our other objectives were to develop students' understandings of unit-related vocabulary; to help students identify the engineering problems and solutions embedded in the story; and to identify the materials used to create the designs in the story.

Before reading the book to our classes, we selected vocabulary from *Yi Min's Great Wall* (Engineering is Elementary Team 2005) and posted the words on the class word wall, along with illustrations and other pictures. For example, we showed pictures of the Great Wall of China, which was the setting for the story. One student, whose father was from China, became so excited by the story that she brought in Chinese toys and artifacts to share more about the culture of the story with her classmates. She was more excited about this unit of study than any other in the school year.

We also provided *realia*: real objects that students could see and touch to understand words and concepts. For example, instead of trying to define *clay* with words, we allowed students to manipulate a chunk of clay borrowed from the art room.

Most English language learner students could easily access the word in their first languages; those with no experience with the material could now form a knowledge base. This was also science learning, as students would require firsthand familiarity with clay's properties for use in their designs at the end of the unit.

Later, when we read the story aloud, we re-examined these words in context. This allowed us to reiterate meanings and point out proper usage in Standard English sentences. Exploring language in context helped students make sense of the science and engineering storyline.

Lesson Two:
Materials and Their Uses

The second lesson, conducted during the following day's science period, was aimed at helping students understand the importance of using appropriate materials in technology. An engineer needs to understand the properties of materials to design objects that will meet the particular needs of a situation.

In this 45-minute activity, students were given a selection of different materials and were asked to choose which material would be the most appropriate for performing certain tasks. For example, one group was asked to find the best way to carry textbooks using cloth, string, or wood. They needed to describe how the material could be used appropriately to complete the task (the cloth could be sewn into a backpack, the wood could be made into a small wagon) in the most productive way.

Other groups' tasks included transporting eggs, keeping warm, and cleaning a floor. This activity helped students identify useful properties of materials used in technologies—a key aspect of materials engineering and a skill they would apply to using earth materials in the design challenge.

Lesson Three:
Describing Earth Materials

Next, it was time for a two-session exploration of the science concepts related specifically to the design challenge. Students explored, compared, and described properties of different earth materials: first as dry samples, then mixed with water, and then mixed with each other and water. However, because both of our classrooms included students who need language support, we began the lesson by challenging students to describe the properties of materials that they encountered in their daily lives before moving on to the less familiar earth material mixtures.

To begin, we discussed the meaning of *properties* and synonyms used in other content areas. We immediately connected this conversation to hands-on experiences with materials. For example, while handling different samples, the second-grade students collectively generated adjectives to describe everyday materials, such as pieces of fabric or a piece of tape. We then created and posted an illustrated word bank with picture clues next to the words for the various properties.

We extended student understanding of the words and the materials by applying the words in contexts related to the design challenge. For example, to understand *sticky*, students touched pieces of transparent tape and applied them to different surfaces. Later, when students were working with clay, sand, straw, and wet and dry mixtures of these, we asked "Were any of these materials or mixtures sticky?" "How might stickiness be useful in walls?" These interplays of concept, language, words, and experiences supported both science and literacy learning and prepared students to use this knowledge in a design context; later they would determine that a sticky substance is good for the mortar used to join bricks in a wall.

This time was well spent. Students showed surprise at the textures that resulted from mixing different earth materials with water. The silky smoothness of silt, the comparative rough or smooth qualities of differently sized gravel samples—these are materials with which our students had little experience. Taking the time to help them carefully observe the properties helped learners build an understanding of the diversity of earth materials and the vocabulary related to properties.

With the vocabulary and conceptual understandings firmly in place, we focused on scientifically exploring the potential building materials for the walls. We asked students to draw from their observations of the wet material mixtures and make (and later test) predictions about what properties these mixtures might have after they were formed into blocks and dried. The student teams shared results by completing a class chart—an additional opportunity for communication.

The combination of experience with the materials with an enhanced vocabulary and understanding of properties allowed students to approach the design challenge with an understanding of the engineering design process—asking pertinent questions, brainstorming ideas, planning, creating, and improving.

Lesson Four:
The Design Challenge

We had now built some important scientific understandings of properties and had done so scientifically (systematically making mixtures and reporting their properties). Students were ready to approach the design challenge: Create a prototype of a wall to protect a school garden.

The second-grade class was presented with an imaginary scenario: The teacher had a garden that neighborhood children had accidentally been trampling, and thus the teacher needed to build a small wall around the garden to protect it. Using a doll to represent the trampling children, the second graders could envision the scaled-down prototypes of the walls.

The fourth-grade class drew from its own, true-life misfortune to complete the scenario.

Wild rabbits from the woods surrounding our school had eaten several of our garden plants, which had been planted earlier to attract birds and butterflies. In both classes, students understood the need for a wall and could relate to the imaginary character's need for one.

We established specific criteria for our walls: at least 45 cm long, at least 20 cm tall, and able to withstand the impact of a baseball rolled against the side. (Such criteria were important to emphasize the nature of engineering design as distinct from arts and crafts projects, in which children might build a representation of a wall that might or might not function to meet a specific need.)

Students received rulers and baseballs so that they would know exactly how to test their designs. Each class spent one 45-minute session individually brainstorming solutions and working in groups of four or five students to decide which design to use. They were asked to choose materials that they had worked with in Lesson Three to create their designs; therefore, they discussed their results from Lesson Three to come up with the design they thought would work best.

Students wrote synopses of their progress and designs and practiced verbalizing their thoughts before presenting them. During the design process, students were encouraged to use think-pair-share, in which they develop their ideas individually and discuss them with a partner before presenting to a group, thereby building verbal confidence. They also drew their ideas and organized and shared data. They connected their own experiences to the engineering design process. In short, students learned through a structured combination of experiences and expressions.

Students' designs included bricks of clay and straw mixtures, mortar with clay, and rock-embedded mud. All the while, children discussed, wrote about, and drew what was going on.

After all students or teams had created their designs, the class tested them with the balls and rulers. Once again, students engaged in scientific skills—conducting and interpreting "fair tests"—within an engineering context. Each wall was carefully measured to see if it met the required length and height. Then the baseball was rolled against it to see if the wall could withstand the impact. Then each student or team had a chance to improve the design, based on the wall's performance. This step provided students with important insights into the nature of the engineering design process and provided a critical opportunity to reconsider and refine the science ideas upon which they based their ideas.

Assessment and Evaluation

Given the linguistic challenges some of our students face, we opted against paper-and-pencil tests to assess science understandings. Instead, we used rubrics to implement embedded assessments of students' understanding of the engineering design process. Our rubrics—modified EiE templates—defined leveled evidence of learning in areas such as identifying materials, describing properties, and making predictions about and connections to relevant concepts. We also tracked individual and group progress, comparing it to our objectives.

Additionally, we evaluated students' drawings, diagrams, and final prototypes for evidence of understanding of the whole unit. Finally, we informally assessed individuals' participation, process, and language acquisition.

In the future, we might also compare successive prototypes. Design changes would indicate to what extent students arrive at and use new insights, understand and incorporate test results, and approach their processes systematically.

Reflections

Through the engineering design challenge, our students moved from a simple hands-on *building* experience into content by *designing* the walls. We asked students to think carefully about their walls and why some might perform well. We focused on properties students could identify that would be important for wall materials. Students helped create and define a list of adjectives to describe the materials we would explore and their results.

We observed that student involvement in engineering design units led to their learning valuable and transferable problem-solving skills as well as acquiring a deep understanding of science concepts. We found that students expressed their knowledge of science better and more creatively than we had seen when we taught from other hands-on science programs.

The activities allowed students to gain and demonstrate science understandings and language acquisition in multiple ways. We anticipate incorporating more design challenges into other science units, thus meeting some of our greatest challenges.

Nancy Yocom de Romero teaches fourth-grade bilingual students, and Pat Slater teaches a second-grade inclusion class, both at Barbieri Elementary School in Framingham, Massachusetts. Carolyn DeCristofano is professional development director at EiE in Boston, Massachusetts.

Resources

Engineering Is Elementary Team. 2005. *Yi Min's Great Wall*. Boston: Museum of Science.

National Research Council (NRC). 1996. *National Science Education Standards*. Washington, DC: National Academy Press.

Internet

Engineering Is Elementary
www.mos.org/eie

Connecting to the Standards
This article relates to the following National Science Education Standards (NRC 1996):

Content Standards:
Grades K–4
Standard A: Science as Inquiry
• Abilities necessary to do scientific inquiry
Standard D: Earth and Space Science
• Properties of earth materials
Standard E: Science and Technology
• Abilities of technological design
• Understanding about science and technology

Every Feather Tells a Story

By Debby Chessin and Laura Chessin

For Mr. Kim's fifth-grade students, recess is not just for playing and getting exercise. One spring, he observed a small group of his students near their class bluebird box, examining various bird feathers found on the ground. He joined the group and watched with interest as they shared and talked about each feather on the ground and excitedly exclaimed, "This one looks like a sword," "Check out these cool colors and patterns!" "Let's see that one over there—it looks really fluffy!" and "Who can find the biggest one?"

In today's climate (with fears of bird flu, West Nile virus, mites, and more), you wouldn't want your students picking up wild bird feathers, but you can easily explore birds by using sterilized bird feathers—available at many craft stores and science suppliers (see Internet Resources).

Building on students' natural curiosity, Mr. Kim purchased some feathers for further exploration in the classroom. He was enthusiastic about developing learning experiences to capture and direct their initial observations and questions. Mr. Kim knew that Mrs. Garcia, the elementary art teacher, would enjoy planning an art lesson to incorporate both science and art concepts with direct observations in nature. Together they planned a series of activities to last a week.

Back in the Classroom

The lessons started with questions about birds and feathers. Earlier in the school year, the class had investigated the basic needs and behaviors of animals. They learned about different habitats and how animals could survive only where their basic needs for air, water, and food were met. Students had observed animals, such as mealworms, then identified their body parts and their functions and described the relationship between form and function and the animal's environment. Mr. Kim saw how this discussion of feathers and birds was a natural progression from the earlier lessons. Students gathered around the front table and examined an assortment of feathers. Students brainstormed questions, which were recorded on a flip chart:

- Why are some feathers so much bigger than others?
- Why does this one have stripes? And that one spots? And this one all one color?
- Why is this feather pointy and that one rounder at the end?
- What kind of bird did this feather come from?
- How can a bird fly without one of its feathers?

- What do the bird's feathers do besides help it fly?

Mr. Kim posted the sheet of questions and offered a simple lesson in feather anatomy. Students learned that *contour* feathers include the flight feathers (*remiges*) and tail feathers (*retrices*), and these feathers are also what give the bird its color. They were excited to learn that tiny fibers called *barbs* that stick out of the midrib (*rachis*) can "zip" open for the bird to clean its feathers and "zip" closed afterwards. They also learned that the edge of the feather that touches the wind first is narrower than the opposite end, and the regularly shaped body feathers protect the bird from the weather, sunlight, and physical objects. Some already knew that down feathers were for insulation. Students learned that shape and color and patterns of bird feathers play important roles in survival and reproduction.

Mr. Kim introduced various classifications of birds (ducks, wading birds, small perching birds, raptors) and explained how birds' anatomies suited them to their habitat. Students brainstormed ideas about different birds they had read about or observed in nature, and the class discussed how birds had special types of claws and beaks that helped them eat different types of foods.

A devoted birder himself, Mr. Kim shared his books and field guides and assembled additional educational bird resources to enhance his young naturalists' understanding of bird characteristics and behavior and their relationship with their environment (see Resources).

Going Birding

The following day, Mr. Kim and his students returned to the schoolyard to gather clues and apply their understanding of feathers to how birds behave, survive, and reproduce in their environment. They listened for and watched birds, observing the unique behaviors for each species, such as how they looked when they were flying, what they did on the ground and in the trees, and where they were found—mostly in the trees or on the ground. (If your school does not have a schoolyard containing a bird habitat, consider a field trip to a local park or wildlife center.)

Each student carried a small sketchbook and pencils to record their observations. Mr. Kim brought several field guides. In their notebooks, students recorded words such as *digging, pecking, flying, soaring,* and *perching;* listed colors, patterns, and shapes they observed among the birds; and noted each bird's relative size. After their "field trip," Mr. Kim added their observations to the flip chart. Students were then assigned to small groups based on reading and language skills, ability, and interests and visited several bird-related learning centers in the classroom.

At one center, students carefully observed feather specimens with magnifiers, then sketched and labeled their drawings using a handout about bird anatomy. At a different center, students looked at pictures and drawings of birds and feathers from books. They sketched their favorite bird and wrote a description of color, patterns, shape, and relative size using vocabulary words. At another center, students visited selected websites (see Internet Resources) to research and answer such questions as:

- What is a special kind of bird feather and what is it used for? (tail feathers—used for lift, balance, steering, braking)
- What is the term for the hard central shaft of the feather? (rachis)
- What are the tiny "hooks" on the feather called? (barbs)

Groups recorded their answers on the flip chart paper.

A Natural Collaboration

Next, students creatively expressed their newfound bird appreciation and knowledge in art class. Mr. Kim and Mrs. Garcia had enthusiastically planned a collaborative art project that integrated science and art processes. In the art lesson, students would revisit form and function of different types of feathers by drawing an "imaginary" bird using repetitive shapes and symmetry, color, and patterns to represent the organism in its natural environment. Students were required to explain what the characteristics they depicted revealed about the bird's environment and behavior. Additionally, students would create a fabric collage that reflected what they had learned about birds in science class.

To stimulate students' creativity for this activity, Mrs. Garcia read *Rainbow Crow* by Nancy Van Laan (1989) and *Owl Moon* by Jane Yolen (1987). She also showed them examples of the cutout collages of French Impressionist artist Henri Matisse from the book *A Bird or 2: A Story About Henri Matisse* (Le Tord 1999). Students were asked to draw upon knowledge of bird biology: characteristics of different birds—colors, shapes, and

Figure 1.
Fantastic feather fusn-damentals.

Work together in your small group. Imagine that you are taking a walk and notice a new kind of bird. You don't have a camera so you observe it carefully and draw it. You decide to translate your drawing to a fabric collage of the bird and a "close-up" view of its different feathers. You will use shapes and colors to represent how the bird survives and reproduces and to create a feeling in your collage.

Plan, draw, and talk about your work.

Safety precautions include proper use of elementary scissors and use of school glue only.

1. Think about what your bird looks like. Consider where it lives and what it might look like. On a separate sheet of paper, draw your bird in its habitat.

2. Draw three types of contour feathers from your bird—flight, tail, and body feathers. Label each type of feather and its parts.

3. Translate your drawing to a fabric bird collage. Cut shapes of different colors of fabric and glue to cardboard covered in fabric to show the environment. Use cool or warm colors, symmetrical and asymmetrical shapes, and fabric to show different patterns.

4. On another piece of cardboard, create a fabric feather collage of a flight, tail, and body feather from your bird. Label each type of feather and its parts.

Write about your work. Please use science vocabulary words in your answer.

5. What do the shapes of your bird's feathers tell about how it survives and reproduces?

6. Classify the shapes of your bird's feathers as symmetrical or asymmetrical. How do you know that?

7. What do your bird's colors tell about its environment?

8. What do your bird's colors tell about how it survives and reproduces?

9. Classify your bird's colors as warm or cool. How do the colors create a feeling and tell a story about the bird in its habitat?

sizes, and birds in their habitats of woods, fields, or perhaps water.

In preparation for the art activity, Mr. Kim made copies of a "Fantastic Feather Fundamentals" worksheet (Figure 1) for each pair of students.

Artful Birds

Using their field notebooks for basic ideas on anatomy and scale, the students drew a selected bird with colored pencils, considering the shape of the body, head, wings, and tail and the size of bill and legs.

After completing their drawings and worksheets, students then observed an example of a fabric bird collage and discussed their experiences. It was clear students grasped the big picture of form and function but stumbled with the vocabulary:

- "The wing feathers have to be strong so they won't fall apart when it is flying ... especially the leading edge. I'm not really sure but I think they are called retrices."
- "The bird is very colorful and matches the flower so it is camouflaged from enemies that way."
- "I think the bird is a male ... because it's colorful ... to attract a female ... to scare aware other males."

Next, students drew a picture of what a *remige*, *retrice*, and *body feather* from the bird in a sample fabric feather collage would look like. Then, students made a fabric feather collage of the bird they had drawn earlier. Students were expected to depict at least one bird adaptation correctly, using the research from science class as a guide. Figure 2 shows the rubric used for the assignment.

For example, one student's collage featured a large bird with red feathers perched in a tree with lots of red fruit, showing that the coloration of the bird served as camouflage. Another student's collage depicted a very light blue bird

Figure 2.
Rubric for fabric collage.

2 pts = good job; 1 pt = partially correct; 0 pt = partially correct/not answered

_____ Classified flight and contour feather

_____ Described form and function of flight and contour feather

_____ Used correct scientific vocabulary to convey information

_____ Used varied and appropriate communication forms

_____ Translated drawing to fabric collage

_____ Identified cool and warm colors

_____ Described how choice of colors created a feeling and told a story of the bird in its habitat

_____ Described how colors and shapes represented parts of the bird

_____ Used and identified symmetrical and asymmetrical shapes

_____ Other

Total possible points = 20

with long legs and a long, slender beak walking along an ocean shore. The bird used its long slender beak to dig for food in the sand.

Expansion for All

Mr. Kim and Mrs. Garcia were pleased with the excitement and sustained focus the project generated among the students. Students clearly understood that shape and color and patterns of bird feathers play important roles in survival and reproduction, and that shape, color, and pattern are ways to represent feelings and tell a story about a bird and its habitat.

To expand on the project, Mr. Kim and Mrs. Garcia invited guest speakers from the area office branch of the U.S. Fish and Wildlife Service to share information about protecting and enhancing bird populations and habitat.

They also created a concept web to connect birds and feathers in other ways across the curriculum. For example, they planned to incorporate social studies topics, such as learning about humans' use of feathers—for clothing, warmth, decoration, and ritual—and studying bird fables and mythology from different cultures. In mathematics, they suggested that students collect and analyze observations and perhaps conduct a backyard bird count.

When the project ended, the two teachers displayed students' creations in the hall. Their colleagues and the school principal were impressed with the work. Many teachers expressed interest in collaborating on projects themselves. Mr. Kim and Mrs. Garcia gathered their project resources and samples, assembled them in a notebook, and placed the notebook in the library for other teachers to use in their planning.

The teachers were proud that the project had not only excited students about learning and helped them make connections among content areas but also inspired their colleagues to do the same.

Debby Chessin is an associate professor of elementary education at the University of Mississippi in Oxford, Mississippi. Laura Chessin is an associate professor of communication and design at the Virginia Commonwealth University in Richmond, Virginia. Mr. Kim and Mrs. Garcia are composites of the many teachers the authors have worked with conducting this activity in classrooms and with the Boys and Girls Club of Oxford, Mississippi.

Resources

Koch, M. 1992. *Bird egg feather nest.* New York: Tabori and Chang.

Le Tord, B. 1999. *A bird or 2: A story about Henri Matisse.* Grand Rapids, MI: Eerdmans Books for Young Readers.

National Research Council (NRC). 1996. *National science education standards.* Washington, DC: National Academy Press.

Parsons, A. 1990. *Amazing birds.* New York: Alfred A. Knopf.

Van Laan, N. 1989. *Rainbow crow.* New York: Alfred A. Knopf.

Yolen, J. 1987. *Owl moon.* New York: Penguin Putnam Books.

Internet

The Cornell University Lab of Ornithology Educator's Guide to Bird Study
www.birds.cornell.edu/schoolyard/index.html

An Engineering Marvel: Types of Feathers
www.nhm.org/birds/guide/pg007.html

Great Backyard Bird Count
www. birdsource.org/gbbc

The Natural History Museum of Los Angeles County Bird Site
www.nhm.org/birds/home.html

Connecting to the Standards
This article relates to the following National Science Education Standards (NRC 1996):

Content Standards
Standard C: Life Science
• The characteristics of organisms (K–4)

Tracking Through The Tulips

By Dorothy Davis

Do you remember the song "Tiptoe Through the Tulips?"—kindergarten through second-grade students at Ashland City Primary in Ashland City, Tennessee, now do. It was their theme song as they participated in Journey North, a free, online educational program that enables students to track the blooming of tulips across the country as spring comes to North America (see Internet Resources).

Not only did this unique program provide an exciting opportunity for online learning, but it was also a perfect springboard for age-appropriate plant inquiries for all the students at the school. We "thought tulips" all year from fall through spring, and teachers were thrilled that the inquiries sparked students' enthusiasm for science and developed their knowledge of numerous science-process skills.

Aha! Tulips!

In the fall of 2002, teachers at our school were expressing interest in finding new ways to teach science as inquiry—and I was looking for an interesting plant inquiry for my second-grade students. That November, I attended a Journey North workshop at the Tennessee Science Teachers Association convention and had an "aha" moment: Journey North was the perfect

vehicle to study plants, and not only for my students—it could involve the whole school in science inquiry!

I was quite excited at the prospect, talking up the Journey North idea to colleagues and eventually channeling my enthusiasm into a proposal for a Toyota Tapestry Grant that would provide the funds necessary for a schoolwide tulip investigation that I called "Tracking Through the Tulips."

The idea was to create two tulip gardens on school grounds: a Journey North garden in which students would monitor tulips' growth and report data to the Journey North website and an "Experimental" garden in which students could explore their own "what if? …" questions related to tulips. In addition, during the winter, students at each grade level would conduct age-appropriate investigations on potted tulips they "forced" indoors using grow lights. Through these experiences, all of the students would practice science inquiry, develop understandings of what is necessary for plants to grow, and begin to make connections about temperature, light, and plant growth.

Luckily, our proposal was reviewed favorably, and in March 2003, we were awarded a $10,000 Tapestry grant. The grant enabled the school to purchase computers and printers, tulips and other plant supplies, safety student thermometers, a grow light, an Ohaus triple beam balance, and latitude maps of North America and compasses, and more—basically, everything we needed to get our tulip project off (or rather, in) the ground. Plus, we could keep the project going each year by just buying new tulip bulbs.

Laying the Groundwork

With the grant in hand, the next step was teacher training. In July 2003, I led a professional development workshop at the school explaining "Tracking Through the Tulips," with the project implementation scheduled for Fall 2003. At the training workshop, I showed a Journey North video that introduced the project. Teachers were given a Journey North tracking map, information on planting tulips, national and state standards the project would cover, soil investigation projects, history of tulips and art sheets of Holland, and information and activity sheets of animals and insects that consider tulips a food source. Teachers were excited about participating.

In September, when school began, the 15 teachers at my school were on board with the project and planning numerous tulip investigations they would conduct with their students. The state standards for each grade level guided the kind of inquiries each class would do. The inquiries with kindergarten students would involve learning about the care and growth of the tulip and learning how to read a thermometer. First-grade inquiries would develop those skills but add the skill of measuring the growth of the tulip with a ruler. Second-grade students would conduct more in-depth inquiries—exploring the interrelationship of the tulips with the soil, animals, insects, temperature, and sunlight. They would also track "blooming dates" on a map as the tulips bloomed in North America and report their data online.

In all of the classes, students would examine a halved tulip bulb under a magnifying glass, keep a science journal, and draw pictures to help show what they had learned.

Planting Time

In the fall, the county agricultural extension agent introduced students to the project. Working with each grade level separately, he presented a play with the characters of tulip, water, different kinds of soil, and the Sun demonstrating how these elements work together to make the tulip grow. Then, he did a hands-on demonstration with different kinds of soil and answered questions about how to grow tulips.

Students learned that soil needs to be made of different-size particles so the water can flow through it slowly and the tulip bulb can get plenty of water but not stand in water. The agent sent our soil off to be tested, and we later found out that our soil needed compost to help the tulips grow well.

In November, the garden sites were plowed in preparation for planting. The gardens were near each other, but the "Experimental" garden was shadier than the Journey North garden. Though teachers knew the amount of available light was a factor that would affect the blooming time of the tulips in this garden, we still believed it was important for students to have the opportunity to investigate their "what if" questions to further develop their inquiry skills.

Planting day—November 4—was completed in one day. Parent volunteers used bulb diggers to dig holes for the bulbs in the Journey North garden, which was about 7 m long and 3 m wide. The experimental garden was about half the size of the Journey North garden, and students dug their own holes at different depths according to their "what if" questions. In both gardens, the students marked "their" tulips by inserting a tongue depressor with their names on it into the ground. In the experimental garden, students worked in groups of four, so they had to decide as a group how they would plant their tulips.

Each class had a designated area in the garden and was allotted 30 minutes to plant their bulbs. Before planting, student weighed their bulbs on a balance scale, measured the bulb's circumference, and recorded the data in their science journals. This enabled us to compare bulbs before and after blooming, as students had such questions as, "Will the bulb weigh the same?" "Will it be the same shape?" and "Will it be the same color?"

Then, students planted the tulips. (Make sure all students wash their hands after digging and handling tulip bulbs or any other plant.) In the experimental garden, every tulip was planted with a different "what if" question in mind:

- What if we planted it upside down? (kindergarten)
- What if we cut the tulip in half and planted it? (first grade) and
- What if we placed wood on top of the bulb. Would it still grow? (second grade)

Back in the classrooms, students reported data, such as the date and temperature, to the Journey North website and also recorded this data in their journals along with their questions and how they planted their bulbs.

All of the students also recorded their prediction of when they thought their tulip would bloom; these ranged from March through April. Overall, they thought the tulips in the experimental garden would bloom at the same time as those in the Journey North garden.

Bulb Dynamics

The day after we planted the tulips in the gardens outside, my second-grade students and I continued our investigations indoors by planting tulips in pots. My intention was to have students "force" them to bloom and through this process develop understandings that temperature and light affect blooming time.

Tulips require an approximately two-month cool period, so through November and December the potted bulbs were kept in a refrigerator at my home set at 5°C and kept moist. Then for about two weeks I kept them in my base-

ment at home in front of a window so that they would gradually get used to light and increased temperature and begin to sprout before they were put under the grow light. The temperature was kept at 14°C and they were watered once a week.

By mid-January, the tulips had emerged, so on February 2 I brought the pots back to school and we continued investigating tulips, this time to explore the relationship that sunlight and temperature have on blooming time.

Tulips and Sunlight

"The Pattern of Sunlight on Our Tulips" centered on answering the question, "How can we get our potted tulips to bloom sooner?" meaning before March, the time we predicted our Journey North tulips would bloom.

Together, we determined our investigation question by first reviewing some of the temperature data we had collected so far in our tulip investigations. We looked at graphs of the temperatures at which we had kept our indoor potted tulips (i.e., Nov.–Dec. 5°C; Jan. 14°C; and Feb. 20°C) and graphs of the outside soil and air temperatures that we had recorded for the tulips in the Journey North garden.

Students observed that, in the first part of February, it was cold and there were no signs of tulips emerging in the pots. Then, in the last half of February, it began to get warmer and the tulips began to emerge and grow.

Next, students looked at some things I had distributed to each of them before our discussion began: a potted tulip, a blank February calendar, and a March Farmer's Almanac calendar that predicted the month's weather and detailed each day's sunrise and sunset times.

I asked, "What is the Farmer's Almanac calendar telling us?" Students replied, "The weather—rainy, snowy, and cloudy." I said, "That is true, but what are those phrases really talking about?" I led students to the idea that those terms were referring to the presence of sunlight in addition to the temperature and precipitation. Then I asked students, "Is there any way to tell how long the Sun is out each day?" and I pointed out that the March Almanac calendar tells the sunrise and sunset times each day. "Does anyone notice a pattern?" I asked.

One student said, "The times always change one number."

"Yes, the Sun rises one minute earlier and sets one minute later every day in March. There is more and more sunlight every day in spring."

One student wondered, "If you gave the tulip more light, would it grow faster?"

The question started the class thinking. I asked, "If tulips bloom in March when there is more light than in February, could we give our pots more light using our classroom's grow light and make them bloom faster?" Students were eager to try.

I told students we needed to figure out how much more light the tulips would be getting in March. They began to write the March sunrise and sunset times on their February calendar. They knew now that this was planning their experiment because they would be using these added daylight hours to set the timer on the grow light.

After the grow lights were set, students maintained the plants. Within two weeks, the first potted tulips bloomed—aptly it was February 13, the day of our Valentine party.

Several weeks after the tulips bloomed, we pulled the bulbs up and found "baby" tulips growing from the original bulbs. I explained these are called *bulblets* and that in a few years they might produce their own blooms. Students were excited to see that even though the tulip blooms had withered, there was new life growing under the soil.

Back to the Gardens

Students were thrilled to see the first tulip bloom in our Journey North garden on March 17. We reported this important event to the Journey North website. We used latitude maps of North America to help locate the different cities where the tulips were blooming. Then the students used a different color marker each week to track the blooming of the tulips. Weekly reports from the website helped the students track tulip blooms across the country and look for a pattern to how spring came to the United States.

For example, the tulips bloomed first around the southern coastlines of California, Texas, and South Carolina. Students remembered they had watched a Journey North video and learned the water along the coastline keeps the land warmer and that is why the tulips bloomed first along the coastlines.

Several weeks after our Journey North tulips began blooming, things started happening in the experimental garden, too. Students were walking around their tulips to see if they had emerged. Those who had planted their bulbs under pieces of wood were looking closely around the wood for signs of life. Others saw the daffodils they had planted with their tulips come up around the tulips (when they bloomed, that was a pretty sight). Some were slower than others emerging and those students were getting worried. They were very concerned about their bulbs that were planted really deep or upside down because they had not emerged as quickly as some of the others, but, when they finally emerged and bloomed, students were excited!

Tulips for Inquiry

We assessed student learning throughout the investigations. In students' science journals they wrote their questions, simple experiments, and results and compared and contrasted the indoor and outdoor plants and the Journey North and the experimental gardens. They wrote causes and effects of the different experiments. They drew, measured, weighed, graphed, and put into sequence the growth of the tulip.

In reflecting on our year of tulips, both teachers and students had a wonderful time learning to do "science as inquiry." The more we did, the easier it became. The students' questions kept guiding the project and helped them get involved and have ownership of it. An unexpected outcome from "Tracking Through the Tulips" was that my "wild" second-grade class had become serious "little scientists!"

Dorothy Davis is a second-grade teacher at Ashland City Primary in Ashland City, Tennessee.

Resources

Glattstein, J., and the National Gardening Association. 1998. *Flowering bulbs for dummies.* Chichester, UK: John Wiley and Sons.

National Research Council (NRC). 1996. *National Science Education Standards.* Washington, DC: National Academy Press.

Pranis, E., and J. Hale. 1988. *GrowLab: A complete guide to gardening in the classroom.* Burlington, VT: National Gardening Association.

Internet

Forcing Tulip Bulbs
   www.mrs.umn.edu/pyg/tips/perennials/tip_1502. shtml
Journey North
   www.learner.org/jnorth
Toyota TAPESTY Grant Program
   www.nsta.org/programs/tapestry

Connecting to the Standards
This article relates to the following *National Science Education Standards* (NRC 1996):

Content Standards
Grades K–4
Standard A: Science as Inquiry
• Abilities necessary to do scientific inquiry
Standard C: Life Science
• The characteristics of organisms
• Life cycles of organisms
• Organisms and environment
Standard D: Earth and Space Science
• Objects in the sky
• Changes in Earth and sky

Section 2

Beyond the School Building Walls: Using Local Sites

Beyond the School
Building Walls
Using Local Sites

Many of the opportunities in this section are literally just outside your classroom door. Using an area that is familiar to students can bring surprises and a new appreciation for their surroundings.

Before taking students out of doors, be sure you have appropriate permission to do so. Some school systems require parent notification or permission even if you are staying on campus for your study. Plan this as you would any field trip considering safety precautions, additional adult help, and requiring students to wear appropriate attire.

Educators in Great Britain have studied the importance of using surrounding school grounds as learning opportunities for many years. Their research provides a lesson in the importance and ease in using the school surroundings for study (Fieldwork Knowledge Library 2003). Education Minister Stephen Twigg referenced this research when he spoke at National School Grounds Week Launch in 2003:

> School grounds are part of a "hidden curriculum" that influences children's attitudes and behavior in a variety of ways and we need to ensure that these are positive influences. Schools which use and have developed their grounds report a number of benefits in addition to their use as an educational resource and improvement to the quality of the school environment. These include

- improved relationships between pupils and staff
- improved relationships with parents
- enhanced image and greater popularity with the local community
- reductions in the incidents of bullying, accidents, and vandalism
- more effective teaching and learning
- development of an ethos of care and a stronger sense of ownership
- more efficient use of existing resources

The advantages of doing some scientific fieldwork on the school grounds include

- familiar to the pupils (less threatening)
- always available and minutes from the classroom so allows regular activities
- can be easily rearranged if it rains
- near to toilets and facilities for washing hands
- no transport need be arranged
- low financial cost
- fitting into normal science time
- regular, long-term field investigations can be done, such as observing seasonal change
- improvement of the school grounds by planting trees, setting up bird feeding stations, managing hedges and creating ponds.

In This Section *(articles are in italics)*

Math and science blend in an integrated outdoor exploration as described in *A Geometric Scavenger Hunt*. This is an easily implemented teaching strategy that can be modified to become a part of every student's experience. The scavenger hunt takes place on the school grounds—no special arrangements, no buses, not a long trip to the site. Just a walk out of the school doors and a field study can take place.

Neighborhoods near the school are excellent resources. *Urban Bird-Watching II* provides suggestions for developing a weeklong activity that enables students to identify a variety of birds found in their local surroundings by using observation skills and identification of characteristics. As they conduct their study, students work in a manner that parallels that of a science researcher.

These Pictures Are Worth a Thousand Words may encourage you to go beyond the school grounds and your neighborhood and see the surroundings in a new way. It provides an unusual technique to use the outdoors as a part of an assessment strategy. It's clear, if you use this type of assessment, students will be eager to take the test.

Nearly every town has a cemetery. This rich resource can provide many interdisciplinary activities. Two articles consider use of this type of site for different outcomes. *Science and History Come Alive in the Cemetery* will jumpstart your thinking about ways in which you might use this site in your teaching regardless of the grade level of your students. This is a multidisciplinary approach blending history and science through firsthand observation and inference. *Cemeteries as Science Labs* looks at cemeteries as outdoor museums. It provides young researchers with valuable archeological and geological information. Step-by-step information—including securing permission from public works or private agencies for the visit, being sensitive to students who may have recently experienced the death of a loved one, activities to conduct on site, and extensions—assures the success of the trip. Sample data record sheets are also provided.

The last article in this section depends heavily on the location in which you live—its climate and physical features. Snow is compared to rock layers in *Snowbank Detectives*. This article provides all of the background information you may need to start your own investigations of snowbanks. The rubrics used to score student work are included to help you from planning through assessment.

References

Organisation for Economic Co-operation and Development (OECD). 1998. "PEB Conference on the Use of School Grounds for Learning." *The Journal of the OECD Programme on Educational Building* 33: 11. Accessed 1/28/2008 at *http://www.oecd.org/dataoecd/17/23/1821406.pdf*.

Fieldwork Knowledge Library: The site for professional fieldwork and outdoor science. 2003. *Using school grounds.* Accessed 1/28/2008 at *www.fieldworklib.org/asp/content.asp?type=c&cat=1&ks=2&id=16*

Resources

The articles listed are available through the Learning Center on the NSTA website at *http://learningcenter.nsta.org*.

Bodzin, A., and L. Shive. 2004. Watershed investigations. *Science Scope* 27: 21–23.

Craven, J., and T. Hogan. 2006. Beachcomlbing for fossils. *Science Scope* 30: 66–69.

Heins, E. D., K. Piechura-Couture, D. Roberts, and J. Roberts. 2003. Parknerships are for all. *Science and Children* 41: 23–29.

Schmidt, P., J. Schumaker Chaddie, and M. Buenzli. 2003. Snow entomology. *Science and Children.* 41: 40–45.

Shields, C. 2004. The adventures of the bucket buddies. *Science and Children* 41: 30–34.

Smith, M. J. 2003. Eyes on the planet: exploring your local watershed. *Science Scope* 27: 36-39.

Thomas, J. 2002. How deep is the water? *Science and Children* 40: 28–32.

A Geometric Scavenger Hunt

By Julie Smart and Jeff Marshall

Children possess a genuine curiosity for exploring the natural world around them. Despite new playground equipment and a renovated kickball field, my third graders still gravitate to an outdoor area teeming with vines and other plant life. Warnings to watch out for spiders or other unexpected creatures seem only to pique their interest further to discover the wilds.

One afternoon as I watched my students exploring during recess, I began wondering how I could get them to study mathematics or language arts with a similar enthusiasm. As we lined up, one of my students hurried to bring me a sweet gum ball she had found in the woods, exclaiming "Look, Mrs. Smart! It's a sphere just like the one we learned about in math!" As the other children crowded around to see her find, one of my students asked a question that would lead us into a four-lesson inquiry investigation that integrated mathematics and science. He asked, "Mrs. Smart, do you think there are more shapes in the woods?" We were about to find out.

Engaging Students

As my students marveled at the sphere-from-the-woods, I began to see a way to spark student engagement in geometry. My students had already completed a unit of study on geometric concepts in math. During our geometry unit, I had provided many application-based learning activities such as exploring geometric features of our school and designing miniature buildings using specific combinations of geometric figures. However, my third graders still seemed to view geometry concepts as isolated and irrelevant to their daily lives. Integrating science and math in this activity provided an opportunity for my students to apply their knowledge of geometry to real-world situations and extend those mathematical concepts to a new context.

To begin the investigation, I posed a question to the class that was similar to the one the student asked while outside: "Do you think there might be more geometry in the woods?" Hands shot up in the air as students volunteered other examples of possible geometry finds waiting to be discovered in our schoolyard habitat. One student suggested we might find leaves shaped like triangles and another guessed there may be sticks to represent line segments.

After brainstorming as a class for 15 minutes, each student took a few minutes to record their predictions and reflect on the day's events in their science journals. I was excited at how engaged my students had become in this endeavor, so I planned to dedicate a second lesson to exploring the environment around our school in what my students had already dubbed, "A Geometric Scavenger Hunt." I followed district guidelines for outdoor field trips, which involved addressing these considerations: parental permission; number of chaperones; medical issues such as student allergies, sunscreen, medications, etc.); appropriate clothing, such as long pants, long-sleeved shirts, and closed-toe shoes; communications, such as available cell phone/two-way radio in case of an emergency; and a review of site to establish it is clear of hazards, including poisonous plants, insects such as ticks and mosquitoes, and man-made hazards such as trash and broken glass.

As my students packed up to go home that day, I overheard several lively conversations about the pending Geometric Scavenger Hunt. It had taken a while, but my students were finally hooked on geometry.

Exploring Nature Using Geometry

For our second lesson, the exploration phase of our investigation, I divided students into teams of three. I explained that students would be using disposable cameras to document their work (one camera would be provided per group). In an effort to maximize potential learning and to keep students focused, each student was assigned one of three roles on the team: photographer, responsible for taking photographs of geometry in nature; scribe, responsible for documenting the justification for each photo; or manager, responsible for having a list of geometry terms and for keeping the group on-task during the activity. After assigning teams and roles, I explained each job and made sure that students understood their individual responsibilities before proceeding.

Before leaving the classroom, we reiterated a few key safety issues. First, I indicated the areas where students could explore, which included only areas inside the school property where students would be in my visual range at all times. Although I had already checked for hazards, as a precaution, I showed photos of several poisonous plants that are native to

our area and reiterated that students were not to handle these plants nor were they to ever eat any berries or other plant parts. I also reminded students to be mindful of sharp or pointed objects like branches. Finally, I told students they were not allowed to go into any overgrown areas, which could be home to snakes or other creatures. The students were ready to begin the investigation.

Students quickly scattered around the schoolyard as they found and photographed examples of geometry in the plant life around them. Students identified and photographed leaves that were symmetrical, branches that formed acute angles, cylindrical logs, and flower petals flecked with miniature line segments. One group of students pointed out an abandoned bee's nest containing hexagonal chambers, and I photographed it; another group observed wild berries exemplifying spheres.

The effectiveness of teamwork was evidenced by the ownership each child took regarding the assigned task. As I circulated among the teams, I saw students making insightful observations, using their knowledge of geometry coupled with their skills relating to scientific inquiry. One student observed, "The veins on this leaf come together to form acute angles." I overheard another student comment on the abandoned bee's nest: "The chambers in the nest are all shaped like hexagons, and they're also the same size so that makes them congruent."

Following approximately 30 minutes of exploration, we returned to the classroom. Students washed their hands with soap and water and checked their clothing for ticks and then began writing reflections of the exploration in their science journals. The use of reflective journaling was an essential component of this investigation. At the end of each lesson, I provided a writing prompt that encouraged students to examine their own thought processes pertaining to the connections between geometry and nature. The prompt for the second lesson read, "What did I learn today that helps me think about geometry in a different way?" One student responded, "I used to think that geometry was just shapes and lines, but now I see that I can find geometry in the world if I look for it. I know how to name the shapes when I see them on paper, and now I can find them when I see them in real life." This student was becoming aware of his ability to identify geometric figures in a new context. Reflective journaling is a method of chronicling this process of metacognitive growth (Hubbs and Brand 2005).

At the end of the second lesson, I gathered the disposable cameras in order to have the film developed that evening, so students would then be able to view their team's photographs the next day and provide a rationale for their geometric classification of items found in nature.

Explaining Our Findings

At the beginning of the third lesson, I distributed each group's photographs and gave the teams an opportunity to match the photos with their notes from the previous day. Teams then began to share their findings and offer geometric justification for their photographs. Students from other teams questioned and in some cases challenged their reasoning for selecting each item. For example, one student disagreed that a team's classification of a photographed log providing an example of a cylinder because it did not have a circular face on both ends; one end was circular, but the other end was conical or pointed. Eventually, the class decided to exclude the object because it lacked the properties of a cylinder that were learned earlier in the geometry unit.

Other similar discussions helped students to confront misconceptions regarding geometric shapes and figures seen in the natural world. One student had photographed a long stick and labeled the object a line. During our discussion, a classmate commented that a line "has to extend infinitely in both directions, and the stick has definite end points." The original student then decided to reclassify the stick as a *line seg-*

ment. Another student shared a photograph of a flower that was missing several petals. She commented, "I can tell that this flower used to be symmetrical, but several of its petals have fallen off. Now it doesn't have any lines of symmetry." A classmate then observed that, if several more petals were strategically removed, the flower would once again be symmetrical. This process of class discussion helped students to make clear distinctions between geometric figures and their properties.

At the conclusion of the third lesson, students again wrote a reflection in their science journals about the day's activities answering the following prompt: "Write about a time during today's class discussion that you did not agree with a group's classification of their photograph. Did you change your mind after hearing the group's explanation?"

Linking to the Animal Kingdom

As the third lesson drew to a close, students began wondering about animals and their geometric traits. Having recently concluded a science unit on animal species, adaptations, and habitats, my students were curious to explore representations of geometry in the animal world as well. I incorporated an online extension activity as a fourth lesson. Students explored geometric features in the animal world using several kid-friendly animal webquests *(www.bestwebquests. com; www.webquest.org)*. Each student individually explored these links to observe a wide array of animal species.

Once again, students were responsible for recording their observations about geometry in the animal world and justifying their classification of geometric elements. Students observed circular patterns on a cheetah's coat, the cone-shaped barb on a stingray, the symmetry of birds' wings, and the triangular teeth of the great white shark. Perhaps the most interesting observation came from a student who observed that an anaconda unhinges its jaw to form an obtuse angle in order to consume its prey whole.

This student went on to explain that most other animals are capable of opening their jaws only into an acute angle.

Other students also made inferences that much of the geometry found in the animal world is very adaptive and functional for the animal. During our class discussion following the webquest, students pointed out how some geometric patterns on animals help to camouflage them in their natural habitat for protection from predators. One student noted the importance of the symmetry of bird and butterfly wings in the animals' ability to fly, and another mentioned the significance of sharp triangle-shaped canine teeth for carnivores. An overarching theme of "functionality" emerged as we discussed the examples of geometry discovered in the animal world.

At the conclusion of the fourth lesson, students wrote a final reflection in their science journals about their experiences with the webquest. As a final extension activity, students were given the choice of creating either a PowerPoint presentation or a poster to highlight several of their findings from the four-day investigation. This open-ended activity provided an opportunity to differentiate by both ability and interest, which has been shown to increase student motivation in the classroom (Tomlinson and McTighe 2006).

Assessment

In an attempt to authentically assess student work for these activities, I developed a performance rubric to accommodate the various formative learning aspects of the investigation. Each component was evaluated on a scale from 1 (incomplete or missing) to 5 (exemplary). The components evaluated included: performance in the assigned role during the outdoor investigation and subsequent team presentation, thoroughness of science journal reflection responses with both science and mathematics concepts, and the correct identification of multiple geometric figures associated with the

second lesson and the webquest portions of the investigation. The student's overall score was then converted into a percentage of the total points available.

Overall, this investigation allowed students to view nature through a different lens, a geometric lens. In the days that followed our investigation, students continued to make insightful observations about the geometric figures they saw all around them. Geometry was no longer just an isolated concept in their math books; rather, it provided a tool that allowed them to examine their world in a completely different way.

Julie Smart is a third-grade teacher in the Greenville County School District in Greenville, South Carolina, and a doctoral student in Curriculum and Instruction at Clemson University in Clemson, South Carolina. Jeff Marshall is an assistant professor of science education, also at Clemson University.

References

Hubbs, D. L., and C. F. Brand. 2005. The paper mirror: Understanding reflective journaling. *Journal of Experimental Education* 28(1): 60–71.

National Research Council (NRC). 1996. *National Science Education Standards*. Washington, DC: National Academy Press.

Tomlinson, C. A., and J. McTighe. 2006. *Integrating differentiated instruction and understanding by design*. Alexandria, VA: Association for Supervision and Curriculum Development.

Connecting to the Standards

This article relates to the following National Science Education Standards (NRC 1996):

Science Education Program Standards
Standard C

The science program should be coordinated with the mathematics program to enhance student use and understanding of mathematics in the study of science and to improve student understanding of mathematics.

Urban Bird-Watching II

By Barbara Rodenberg

I n "Urban Bird-Watching," previously published in *Science Scope,* I described an activity designed to get students out of the classroom and into the outdoors (Rodenberg 1993). In that activity, I suggested ways to familiarize students with urban, rural, woodland, and river habitats as well as common birds of Eastern cities. This activity continues the outdoor theme by exploring bird populations and ecosystems. Students use math and probability to analyze differences in counts of three species of birds. Students also analyze the role of an introduced species, the European starling, in the urban environment.

Natural Questions

During the first Urban Bird-Watching activity, my students wondered why they saw many birds of the *same* species in the urban environment, as opposed to birds of many different species in the rural environment. Specifically, why were there so many starlings near the school?

To answer this question we set out in neighborhoods near the school to see if we could document our preliminary, qualitative observations—thus began Urban Bird-Watching II. We counted the numbers of starlings (*Sturnus vulgaris*), robins (*Turdus migratorius*), and cardinals (*Cardinalis cardinalis*) seen or heard from 10 different points along a one-kilometer transect route. Then we analyzed the data to determine if, statistically, there really were more starlings than other types of birds. Using these results, we launched into a discussion of introduced species and their effects on urban environments.

By the end of this weeklong activity, students are able to identify cardinals, robins, and starlings by sight and sound; define *introduced species* and *crevice organism;* and participate in discussions about introduced species. Procedural objectives include participating in the transect count, keeping a data sheet, sharing information with classmates, and calculating chi-squared statistics. To complete the activity successfully, students must work cooperatively in groups to determine the transect routes, measure and mark off segment points, collect and discuss data, and prepare an oral report on an introduced species.

Materials

For each group, I provide a field equipment kit from supplies at school. Each kit contains a pair of binoculars, a copy of Roger Tory Peterson's *A Field Guide to the Birds,* a clipboard, a pencil, a meterstick, a stopwatch, a street map, sidewalk chalk, and carpenter's chalk (for grass). In the classroom, you will need an audiotape of songs and calls of the three species, calculators, and a copy of the article "Starlings Are No Darlings."

One Day at a Time

On the first day, I explain the main points of the activity. I organize students into groups of three; have each student choose to be the Leader, Counter, or Recorder for their group; and distribute an equipment kit to each group. Then, I review the identification characteristics of cardinals, robins, and starlings (learned in "Urban Bird-Watching") and have students write brief descriptions of each species based on the information in the field guide.

On the second day, I play the audiotape to teach the birdsongs of these three species. Students enjoy learning by imitating the sounds. Then I have groups go outside with their meter-sticks to practice pacing and marking off 10-m segments. This exercise helps students develop a uniform pacing technique, so metersticks won't be needed during the transect counts.

On the third day, students map out one-kilometer transect routes in neighborhoods near the school and perform the transect counts. (If the proposed routes are near roads, remember to address safety issues before starting out.) If I have enough adult assistance, each group walks its own route. If I have only one assistant, I lead the first group in pacing and marking a route, the other groups follow three minutes apart on the same route, and the assistant accompanies the last group. At each 100 m mark the groups count and record the number of birds of each species seen or heard in a one-minute period of time. In addition to each student keeping track of one species throughout the count, the Leader paces and marks off each 100 m segment, the Timer keeps track of the time, and the Recorder writes down the data.

The transect counts take one full class period to complete. Although the segments are far enough apart to eliminate most overlap-ping counts of the same birds, you may want to address this point later in class as a possible weakness of the experiment design.

The next day, each group analyzes the pooled class data to determine if the differences between the numbers of each species are statistically significant. Students follow the step-by-step instructions in the student activity sheets (Figure 1). Moving from group to group, I coach and facilitate the group work and discussions. Students may have fabricated data to avoid recording zeroes in their data sheets; I discuss how this can affect the whole class's data.

The chi-squared test is used by scientists to determine if the observed data values differ significantly from expected values. In this activity we compare the observed numbers of the three species with the mean value of all three species to see if they differ. (We use the mean as the expected value because we expect to see equal numbers of all birds.)

On the last day of the unit, I begin with a class discussion designed to show that there are more starlings than robins and cardinals near the school. I focus the discussion with questions such as

- Are there any patterns in the data?
- Were there any segments with a count of zero for all birds?
- What might account for a zero count? (*sudden loud noises, traffic*)
- How would these factors affect the quality of the habitat over the long term?

Before class, I separate "Starlings Are No Darlings" into five to seven sections of four to six paragraphs each and glue each section onto a piece of card stock. After the first discussion I hand out one section of the article, a blank overhead transparency, and a water-soluble, overhead pen to each group. Each group determines and writes down the main idea of its section. I arrange the groups' transparencies in proper sequence and use them to guide our discussion. At the end of this discussion, students should know that starlings are an introduced species that have found a niche. I summarize by defining *niche, introduced species,* and *coevolution.*

I have students look at the distribution map of starlings in the back of the Peterson Field Guide to determine how the range of starlings has expanded across the country from New York City in the last century. Then individual students choose another introduced species to write about in a report to be presented to the class. Possible choices include the water hyacinth, zebra mussel, kudzu, house sparrow, or purple loosestrife.

Bird's-Eye View

I assess each student's performance with the student activity sheets. A short summary evaluation can be used as well. You may want to use multiple-choice or essay questions about the three bird species, their ranges, and their habitats.

Middle level students enjoy having a say in the activity design, working in groups, and learning outside. I often hear comments such as "Now this is really doing science" and "So this is what scientists do!"

Barbara Rodenberg is an assistant professor in the Department of Education at Columbia Union College in Takoma Park, Maryland.

References

Peterson, R. T., and V. M. Peterson. 1988. *A field guide to the birds: A completely new guide to all the birds of Eastern and Central North America.* 4th ed. Boston: Houghton Mifflin.

Rodenberg, B. 1993. Urban bird-watching. *Science Scope* 18 (7): 12–17.

Walton, R. K., and R. W. Lawson. 1999. *Backyard bird song.* Boston: Houghton Mifflin.

Lawren, B. 1990. Starlings are no darlings. *National Wildlife* 28 (3): 24–27.

Resources

Ambrose, K. 1995. *A handbook of biological investigation.* Knoxville, Tenn.: Hunter Textbooks.
Garber, S. D. 1978. *The urban naturalist.* New York: John Wiley and Sons.

Figure 1.
Student activity sheet.

Day 1. Preparation
1. Look up the American robin, northern cardinal, and European starling in your field guide. Write a brief description of each bird. Are males and females similar?
2. Decide who will be your group's Leader, Recorder, and Timer.
3. Pick up a field equipment kit from your teacher.

Day 2. Practice
1. Your teacher will play an audiotape of robin, cardinal, and starling songs and calls. Listen carefully and imitate them to learn the characteristics and be able to identify the birds by ear.
2. In the parking lot, use the meterstick to measure 10 m.
3. Mark both ends of this distance with chalk.
4. Practice pacing off the distance.

Figure 1.
Student activity sheet continued.

5. Count the steps needed for each of you to pace 10 m.
6. Record your number of steps:

_____

Number of steps in 10 m_____ x 10
= _____ steps in 100 m (one transect segment).

Day 3. Transect counts
1. Organize your group and get your field equipment kit.
2. Review the identifying characteristics of robins, cardinals, and starlings. Have each group member choose a species to count throughout the transect.
3. Choose a 1-km transect near the school and mark it on your map with a highlighter.
4. The Leader paces and marks off each 100-m segment along the 1 km transect, using the number of paces determined during the practice session. The Timer and Recorder follow. Stop at the end of each segment and count the number of birds seen or heard for a period of one minute. During this period the Timer keeps track of the time and the Recorder writes down the data.

Day 4. Data analysis
1. Add up the total number of each species your group recorded throughout the transect.
2. Share your totals as your teacher writes down all groups' totals on the overhead.

3. Which species accounted for the greatest percentage of birds observed?
4. Draw a pie graph to show each species' percentage in the total number of birds recorded by the class.
5. Discuss reasons for the differences in the numbers of each species counted. List them.
6. Check the information about these species in the field guide. Brainstorm hypotheses as to why the numbers are different.
7. Are the differences in the numbers statistically significant? Do a chi-squared test to find out.
   (a) mean for all three species: _____
   (b) chi-squared formula:

$$X^2 = \frac{(\text{observed} - \text{expected})^2}{\text{expected}}$$

summed over all species.

observed = total number of robins (then cardinals, then starlings)
expected = mean of three species' recorded totals
(c) fill in the numbers on the following chart.

species	observed	expected	$(o-e)^2/e$
robin			
cardinal			
starling			
			X^2 (sum)_____

Figure 1.
Student activity sheet continued.

(d) X^2 must be greater than the *critical value* for the differences among the species to be statistically significant. Use the following chart to find the appropriate critical value for this experiment. The *degrees of freedom* is one less than the number of groups (species) in the data set. The degrees of freedom for this experiment is _____

df	critical value
1	3.84
2	5.99
3	7.81
4	9.49
5	11.1

The critical value for this experiment is _____
X^2 is greater than   less than the critical value. (circle one)

8. According to these calculations, is the difference in the number of birds in each species statistically significant?
Optional: Verify your pie graph and chi-squared test by entering your data into a spreadsheet program and printing the results.

Day 5. Discussion
1. Read the assigned section of the article "Starlings Are No Darlings" out loud in your group. Determine the main idea of the section and write it down.
2. Take notes on other important details from your group's discussion.
3. Listen as other groups present the main idea and details from their sections. Take notes.
4. Go back to question three in day four and review the reasons your group listed. What do you think now?
5. So far, you have been working in a group to do this study. Think about all the work you have done and write an individual report on another introduced species. You may use outside sources as long as you include them in a reference list. You will be graded on the scientific content, organization, reference list, and use of language.

These Pictures Are Worth a Thousand Words

By Roberta Schempp

The cameras are loaded, the Sun is out, and my students are at the park to take their year-end science final. Yes, at the park, with cameras. The paper and pencils will come a little later, but right now, their brain waves are really going. They are having fun at the park, enjoying the sunshine, and showing me what they have learned over the past year. They are also getting some exercise and fresh air, which is just an added benefit to this picture-perfect final exam.

Now that I have piqued your interest, let me explain. All year, my class has been working hard. In December, they had to take midyear finals, and they certainly are not looking forward to another round of them, especially now that spring fever has set in. However, they are looking forward to their science final. It's a beautiful day outside, and that is where I take them.

Present the Hypothesis

About a week before their science final, I present the class with a hypothesis: "I think you have learned something in science this year."

Then, I tell them that their assignment is to prove the hypothesis true. I divide them into small groups of three to five students and ask them to review what they learned during the past year by thumbing through their texts and notes and recording all of the major topics that we covered. During this review, each group puts together a list of at least 30 possible science concepts that it could illustrate with a photograph taken at the park.

Send Them Outside

I purchase one disposable camera for each group (see Resource). On the day we go to the park, I take a group picture of the entire class with each group's camera. After discussing safety and proper behavior, I give one disposable camera to each group and remind them that the goal is to cover as many concepts as possible, not to worry about the exact number of photos they take. Then I send them on their way. They have 90 minutes to use their roll of film and return to a preset meeting place.

Encourage Creativity

The possibilities for subject matter are endless, especially if you encourage your students to be creative. For example, when one group of students had trouble finding a frog to photograph, they decided to snap a shot of students playing leapfrog instead. Also, you can suggest that they use more than one photo to illustrate dynamic concepts, such as the change of seasons, regeneration, and chemical and physical changes. One drawback is that students tend to focus on plant and animal life, and they avoid finding chemistry and physical science subjects to photograph. You may want to require photographs from each discipline to avoid this problem.

Album Construction

After the photo shoot, I take the film to be developed and I order two copies of each picture at a place where the second print is always free. When the pictures are developed a few days later, I return the prints to each group. I allow them to divide one set of prints among themselves as souvenirs of their seventh-grade science final. Each group uses the second set of prints to create a photo album that they will present to the class as their science final.

Each group's photo album must include photo captions that fully explain each picture and the science topic it shows. When I grade the photo album, I grade the accuracy of the information in the caption. For instance, in the leapfrog example, a group could earn points for explaining the stages of metamorphosis, the meaning of *amphibia*, or the number of chambers in the hearts of different animals. Additionally, I assess each album for creativity and whether or not the group proved the hypothesis, "I think you have learned something in science this year."

Picture-Perfect Presentation

We mount the photos and captions on construction paper, laminate each page with the school's laminating machine, and bind each album with a comb binder. We do our presentations on the last full day of school at the end of the school day and invite the parents so they can find out what their children learned during the past year. Some parents are unable to attend, but we try to notify them well in advance so they can take off work if needed. Some parents take off early because it's the last day of school and they come to help their children take home the contents of their desks and lockers.

The main benefit of this activity is that the students enjoy this type of final and, as a result, spend quite a bit of time on it. They are allowed to pick their own topics, which creates motivation and a sense of ownership. Best of all, it is something different—and by the end of seventh grade, they deserve something out of the ordinary.

Roberta Schempp is a science teacher at Hope Lutheran School in Shawnee, Kansas.

Resource

The cost of camera purchase and film development was approximately $4 per student (in 2001). Because this activity was considered one of their field trips, these costs came out of the student activity fund.

Science and History Come Alive in the Cemetery

By Patricia K. Lowry and Judy H. McCrary

City cemeteries are often very old, with gravestones dating back to the early 1800s. Some of the markers are carved out of rocks and may be quite simple, containing only names of the deceased and dates of birth and death; others contain no information at all. This is in sharp contrast to some of the very elaborate markers carved out of granite with intricate designs and embellishments that we see today.

A visit to the cemetery coincides with the National Science Education Standards, which advocate developing an understanding about scientific inquiry using different types of investigations. Specifically, it involves developing questions, forming an explanation, and then describing the results.

A trip to the cemetery can be conducted as either a field trip or as a homework assignment. Students are given a guide with questions addressing issues as they pertain to science and history (see Figure 1). After receiving a self-guided map, students progress at their own speed. During the tour, the students investigate reasons for various observable phenomena. For example, students theorize about why they see tilted markers and sunken graves, providing explanations such as, "The ground has settled over the years due to erosion and rain," or, "Erosion has caused the markers to sit at an angle." Another investigation area involves the surface of the stone markers. A final observation involves identifying specific plants in the cemetery. In addition, back in the classroom, scientific and historical explanations can be investigated through related hand-on discovery opportunities.

History

A trip to the cemetery can further science learning and interdisciplinary connections as well. Specifically, historical concepts can be investigated throughout the walking tour. These concepts include finding information about individual family units, birth and death records, health issues, and specific events in history. For example, our trip to the cemetery yielded information about infant mortality rates, signers of the Declaration of Independence, Civil War soldiers, slaves, and causes of death.

51

Figure 1.
Cemetery walking tour.

Science elements
1. Why are some of the markers tilted?
2. Examine the surface of a stone. What do you notice about the texture? How legible is the writing? What natural forces act on the stones?
3. Why are some of the graves sunken?
4. Name some of the plants or wildflowers that you see growing here (adapted from Hansen 1989).

History elements
1. Write down interesting inscriptions from headstones.
2. Write down the names of the infants (birth to three years) that you saw as you walked along. Record years of life.
3. Did husbands generally survive their wives or did wives outlive their husbands?
4. Did occupation, if it is provided, seem to affect the age of death? How and why?
5. Do a rubbing of an interesting tombstone (adapted from Chapin and Messick 2002).

Conclusion

Learning experiences are important both inside and outside of the classroom. A walking tour of a local cemetery is an excellent way to allow students the opportunity to connect with the community's past while at the same time providing a successful collaborative curriculum experience with history.

Patricia K. Lowry is a professor of education and Judy H. McCrary is an associate professor of elementary education at the Jacksonville State University in Jacksonville, Alabama.

References

Chapin, J. R., and R. G. Messick. 2002. *Elementary social studies: A practical guide.* 5th ed. Boston: Allyn & Bacon.

Hansen, K. L. 1989. Tombstones as textbooks. *Learning* 18 (3): 27–29.

National Research Council (NRC). 1996. *National Science Education Standards.* Washington, DC: National Academy Press.

Cemeteries as Science Labs

By Linda M. Easley

Cemeteries can be outdoor museums, teeming with valuable information that tells a story. They provide archaeologists with an opportunity to examine how artifacts (tombstones and monuments) reflect cultural change and how societies differ from one another. Archaeologists can record information about the size, shape, symbols, and weathering of the grave markers. They record information about the people buried in the graves and look for patterns. Preservation of cemeteries is a point of national interest at this time, with research dollars being distributed to local agencies.

A trip to a local cemetery can also be an opportunity to engage students in real-world science, emphasizing the process and nature of science. It can even be a costless trip when the graveyard is within walking distance from the school. Exploration of a cemetery provides connections to mathematics, social studies, language arts, and archaeology.

Before visiting the cemetery with students, we conduct a 30-minute, in-class activity that simulates the weathering of tombstones using sidewalk chalk (see Figure 1). The materials required for this activity are very inexpensive and can be gathered easily. Aprons are a necessity because bleach can ruin clothing. Students should wear safety glasses because the bleach and vinegar both could hurt the eyes.

You do not have to gain permission to visit public cemeteries, and they are usually well tended and have few safety hazards. Always visit the cemetery before taking your class so that you can look for safety hazards such as unstable stones, exposed roots, depressions in the soil, and erosion; the composition of grave markers (most are granite, marble, or brick, but sandstone and metal are also found); and tombstone symbols, epitaphs, and trends in death dates. I look for a cemetery that contains markers from the late 1800s through the 1900s. If the cemetery is no longer in use or has been

Figure 1.
Tombstone weathering.

Did you know that tombstones and monuments are both physically and chemically weathered? Physical weathering is a result of erosion from rainfall, hail, wind-blown soil, cracking due to changes in temperature, and cleaning and/or rubbing by humans. Chemical weathering is a result of the interaction of chemicals and the material from which the monument is made. In areas that have many industrial plants, acid rain increases the rate of weathering far beyond the usual speed. Cleaning agents such as bleach, detergents, and soaps also speed the rate of weathering. Combinations of chemical and physical weathering, such as acid rain and humans scrubbing with detergents, can double the normal rate of weathering.

In this activity, you will simulate the weathering of tombstones by making a model and exposing it to both physical and chemical weathering. You will draw some conclusions about how weathering affects actual tombstones. In this activity, you will use chalk, which is similar to, although much softer than, limestone and marble, materials once used to make grave markers. The weathering that would take about 25 years in a cemetery will occur immediately with your chalk model.

Materials
- sidewalk chalk
- rubbing paper
- acid rain solution (household vinegar)
- crayons
- bleach solution (1:4 ratio of bleach to water)
- water
- soft drink cans to simulate rain
- pan to catch runoff
- apron to protect your clothes
- plastic knife

Group members
- Materials manager: picks up and returns materials
- Speaker: reports for the group, asks questions
- Recorder: records all information
- Guide: makes sure everyone is following directions and is on task
* Other specific jobs are listed within an activity

Procedure
1. Have your materials manager get two pieces of sidewalk chalk to use as tombstones from your teacher.
2. Use the plastic knife to carve a name, date, or symbol onto your tombstones. Use one of the symbols that you saw in the cemetery on your field trip. Both must be exactly alike. Have your recorder draw a picture of your model tombstones.
3. Have your materials manager get a piece of rubbing paper and a crayon from the materials station.
4. Have your guide hold one piece of the chalk while the speaker places the rubbing paper over the chalk and hold it. Have your recorder make a rubbing of your tombstone.
5. Answer questions 1–3 and have your recorder document your answers.
6. Have your materials manager get a soft drink can, water, the acid solution, the base solution, an apron from the materials station, and safety goggles for each group member.
7. Place the second tombstone in the pan. Fill the soft drink can halfway with water and quickly pour it over the model grave marker. Let all the water flow from the can.
8. Answer question 4. Pour the solution out of the pan.
9. Repeat steps 7 and 8 using first the acid rain solution and then the bleach solution. Complete the remaining questions.

Questions
1. Examine the rubbing you have made. Look at the back of the rubbing paper. What do you notice?
2. Compare the model grave markers. Look at the carvings you made in the pieces of chalk. What do you notice?
3. Describe how making gravestone rubbings causes physical weathering.
4. Describe the weathering due to the rain event you just simulated.
5. Which of the chemical weathering simulations caused the most damage to your model?
6. What do you think would have happened if you had scrubbed the model with the bleach solution?
7. What can you do to prevent chemical and mechanical weathering of monuments and tombstones?
8. What will you tell your friends and relatives about cleaning monuments and tombstones?
9. Make a general statement describing what you learned about weathering of monuments and tombstones from this activity.

used for only the last 50 or so years, trends in tombstone composition are very hard to determine. After the turn of the century, most memorial markers are granite. Before the field trip contact parents to obtain permission for students to attend and to find out if the student has recently experienced the death of a loved one. If that is the case, I work with the parents to make the field trip a positive event for the child. I also ask about family cultural values.

Armed with information gathered in the preliminary visit, I create a scavenger hunt and archaeological study of a cemetery to be completed at the site (see Cemetery studies, pp. 56 and 57). The scavenger hunt evaluates the weathering on tombstones and monuments and the archaeological activity prepares students for what they will see at the cemetery in terms of weathering of stones. Before beginning the activity, everyone should know the difference between marble, granite, concrete, and metal. Marble has very fine grains and is only white to gray. Granite comes in a variety of colors, is often polished, and has large grains. I get samples from a local headstone maker and show them to my class prior to the visit. Students must be given ample time to complete both charts during the cemetery visit. I found that more appropriate data was collected when two group members are assigned to each part of the activity sheet.

It should be noted that environmental conditions affect the weathering of grave markers. Weathering will be increased in areas where there is a lot of wind blowing dirt and sand against the markers. High humidity promotes the growth of biological material on stones and the chemicals released by these organisms contribute to weathering. In areas with wide yearly temperature ranges, the expansion of water freezing in crevices in stones increases weathering. Cleaning of stones with harsh chemicals and brushes also causes increased weathering, more than all natural forces combined. (See Figure 1 for

Figure 2.
Tombstone information.

1979–2004:
Almost all tombstones dated between 1979 and 2004 are granite; a few are marble. Expect these stones to be unweathered to mildly weathered. Brick and concrete monuments should be unweathered. Metal markers will also be unweathered, unless they are copper. The green patina will be present on copper memorials. The green patina may have bled onto the stone marker.

1954–1978:
Granite gravestones tend to be unweathered. Marble monuments usually exhibit mild weathering. Brick and concrete monuments are usually unweathered. Metal markers will also be unweathered, unless they are copper. The green patina will be present on copper memorials. The green patina may have bled onto the stone marker.

1929–1953:
Granite tombstones still predominate this period and are unweathered. The marble tombstones in this era are usually mildly weathered. Brick and concrete monuments are usually mildly weathered. Metal markers may be mildly weathered or unweathered, depending on the metal used.

1904–1928:
The granite stones remain unweathered. The marble markers may be moderately weathered. Brick and concrete monuments are usually mildly to moderately weathered. Metal markers may be mildly weathered, with the green patina present on copper markers. Iron markers will exhibit rusting.

1879–1903:
You may see sandstone grave markers (sand colored), more marble markers, and fewer granite markers. Iron crosses are common during this time period. The sandstone and marble will be moderately weathered. Concrete usually remains only mildly weathered, but brick shows moderate weathering. Granite markers are usually unweathered. Metal markers may be mildly to moderately weathered, with the green patina present on copper markers. Iron markers will exhibit rusting.

1854–1878:
You may see sandstone grave markers (sand colored), more marble markers, and fewer granite markers. Iron crosses are common during this time period. Expect the sandstone, brick, iron, and marble grave markers to be all highly weathered. Granite may be mildly weathered.

Pre-1854:
Expect most markers to be highly weathered, including all metals. No granite markers will be found, as the technology for cutting granite was not developed during this time period. If a granite marker is found, it is a replacement stone.

Cemetery studies

In this activity, you will evaluate the weathering on tombstones and monuments in a local cemetery. You will also collect other data about the graves you observe. The data you collect on site will be analyzed later to determine trends, help uncover historical events, and draw conclusions. Split your group into two pairs to conduct each part of the activity simultaneously. When we return to the classroom, you will combine the information.

Part 1: Scavenger hunt data sheet
Procedure

Find the following items and record your information in the data table. It is important for you to see all these things, as they will be discussed after the scavenger hunt.

Find	Name and date of death	
Stones		
Marble headstone		
Granite headstone		
Metal headstone		
Concrete headstone		
Symbols		**Composition of stone**
Lamb		
Hand		
Organizational symbol		
Stone carver's signature		
Angel		
Historical markers		
Civil War veteran		
World War I veteran		
World War II veteran		
Sailor		
Markers		
Mausoleum		
Box tomb		
Headstone		
Sculpture		
Obelisk		
Bench		
Cross only		

information on tombstone weathering and Figure 2 for guidance on the weathering patterns and composition of markers.)

The students that I have worked with have all been very excited about visiting the cemetery, yet incredibly respectful once they arrived at the memorial park. They busily collected data, sharing with classmates interesting things they found. Almost all indicated that they "never knew that" during the experience. I learned

Cemetery studies

Part 2: Archaeological study of a cemetery
Procedure
1. Describe the location of the cemetery. Is it urban, suburban, or rural? Are there houses nearby? Is there industry nearby?
2. Using the table below as a guide, document five markers for each date span.

Monument weathering data table
  1—Unweathered: face has smooth surface texture; no stains; no pockmarks
  2—Mildly weathered: some wearing of the surface; smooth in some areas, but not others; stained; shallow pockmarks
  3—Moderately weathered: wearing visible on surface; rough surface; stained; inscription still readable; rounded edges; moderate pockmarks
  4—Highly weathered: very rough surface; stained; inscription unreadable or barely readable; deep pockmarks and scarring; very rounded edges

	Name	Year of death	Composition of monument	Degree of weathering
1979–2004				
1954–1978				
1929–1953				
1904–1928				
1879–1903				
1854–1878				
Pre–1854				

3. After completing the table, analyze your data by making a timeline that shows the type of stones used over the period. Write a statement describing what you discovered.
4. On a sheet of graph paper, graphically represent your data. Include the age of the tombstones and the degree of weathering you discovered.
5. Write a statement that describes the relationship between time and the amount of weathering that has occurred in your cemetery.
6. Write a statement that describes the relationship between time and the type of monuments that you found in your cemetery.

that visits to cemeteries are more pleasant when done in late fall or early spring when vegetation is minimal and fewer insects are present. Be sure to take insect repellent and plenty of water along whenever you go.

In class the next day, we go over the answers to the questions and discuss the experience together. You may also choose to include further activities, such as writing a story about the cemetery from the point of view of one of the deceased, or give students a different set of cemetery data to analyze and then answer the same questions.

Extensions

Of course, use of a memorial park is not limited to physical science. Students can evaluate the flora and fauna they find. They can collect leaves from native plants. They can observe animals in their natural environment. Students can employ mathematics skills to find the perimeter and square footage of the park and then determine how many gravesites are available. They can survey the geometric shapes found in the cemetery. Language arts students can read, copy, and analyze epitaphs, then write their own for themselves or a pet. They can write stories about the deceased based on the symbols and epitaphs found. Social studies students can analyze trends in immigration, infer causes of deaths, and compose historic marker verbiage based on their analyses of graveyards. Educational uses of cemeteries are limited only by the teacher's imagination.

Linda M. Easley is a professor of education at Louisiana State University in Shreveport, Louisiana.

Reference
National Research Council (NRC). 1996. *National Science Education Standards. Washington,* DC: National Academy Press.

Resource
National Center for Preservation Technology and Training *www.ncptt.nps.gov*

Acknowledgment
Activities designed by Linda M. Easley and Kimberly Walker McAlister, June 2004. Teacher notes were gleaned from research done by John Thiel, Michigan State University, Spring 1998, and personal visits to cemeteries.

Connecting to the Standards
Abilities necessary to do scientific inquiry:
- Use appropriate tools and techniques to gather, analyze, and interpret data
- Develop descriptions, explanations, predictions, and models using evidence
- Think critically and logically to make the relationships between evidence and explanations

Physical science standards:
- Level 5–8 properties and changes in properties of matter

Snowbank Detectives

By Eric A. Olson, Audrey C. Rule, and Janet Dehm

In our city, located on the shore of Lake Ontario, children have ample opportunity to interact with snow. Water vapor rising from the relatively warm lake surface produces tremendous "lake effect" snowfalls when frigid winter winds blow. Snow piles along roadways after each passing storm, creating impressive snowbanks. When a tractor-mounted snow blower slices through these snowbanks, the succession of snowstorms is revealed as interesting layers of different thicknesses and colors.

As science education professors with an interest in geology, we couldn't pass up the opportunity to study sedimentary processes and phase changes with the mounds of snow right in our own front yards. Our colleague—a fourth-grade teacher at a local school with an abundance of snowbanks—teamed up with us to create this weeklong snowbank investigation.

Sedimentary Snow

Before our snow investigations, students had been studying the three types of rocks: igneous, sedimentary, and metamorphic. Snowbanks, like sedimentary rock formations, are made of sediments deposited from above, creating a layered sequence.

We began the lessons by showing students an electronic slide show of photographs we had taken of snowbanks in neighborhoods around the school. Students immediately noticed the layered patterns of snow and suggested that thicker layers represented larger snowstorms. Students easily made the connection to sedimentary rock layers. One student noted the snowbanks "all have sedimentary rock forms and are lots of dark and light colors." Students' level of interest was high because they already loved snow for its beauty and for the recreation it provided.

Through our observations, we discovered another geology connection: comparing icicles and stalactites.

Explanations for Dark Layers

After the slide show, students worked in small groups to examine the snowbank photographs and record their observations. In order to document their initial understanding, we provided questions to prompt observations and inferences: What features do you notice about the snowbanks? What do you think caused these features? Students, engaged in the inquiry, asked questions of their own: Why is the snow brown? and Why are only some of the snowbanks melted?

Students observed the layers, their different thicknesses, the variety of colors, and the holes or brown spots in the snowbanks. Then students used their previous knowledge to suggest explanations. Many children were not aware that plows push snow mixed with salt and sand up onto the snowbanks, producing the dark, thin layers. Students assumed instead that cars splashed the dirt: "A car might have gone by and put mud on the snow."

Another idea expressed by some students was that salt turned the snow brown. Some students attributed the darkness of the lower layers more to splashing by cars rather than to compaction because of age. It might have made sense to students that lower layers were dark in color for the same reason cars become dirty. It is a more complex idea to consider that the lower layers are darker because of melting of snow, thereby concentrating the amount of dirt and rock.

However, there were students who understood at least part of the process well: "The snowbank starts white and then the plow came by and turned it brown, then it just kept switching brown and white, brown and white."

Changing Snow

During our next class session, we discussed the changing size and shape of snowbanks. We asked students to describe their experiences with snow melting and refreezing. In the morning, they walked over hard snow, but in the afternoon when the Sun was shining, they sank up to their knees. Our students had first-hand knowledge—knowing the "right" snow for snowman construction—with the various forms snow takes. One student noted, "It is easier to make a snowball on the way home after school. The snow is too hard in the morning."

Most students inferred relationships between the condition of snowbanks and the intensity of sunlight shining on the surface. Shade from trees or buildings and the slope of the ground make noticeable differences in the size of the snowpack. "The Sun and the warmth might explain the difference." A student suggested that being "closer to the grass" would have an effect on melting because the grass would soak up the water. To explain size and appearance differences, one student stated, "Snowbanks closer to direct sunlight that have nothing to block it usually melt first."

The Benchmarks for Science Literacy (AAAS 1993) state that "by the end of the fifth grade, students should know that heating and cooling cause changes in the properties of materials" (p. 77). We showed the class two photographs of snowbanks taken on opposite sides of the same street. The larger, lighter-colored bank with distinct, even layers faces north. The shorter, darker bank faces south. The major variable accounting for differences is the amount of sunlight shining on them: The north-facing bank spent most of the day in the shade.

Students were able to understand this abstract relationship more clearly when the next day we took them outside to directly observe snowbanks. We examined snowbanks on the school grounds to find evidence to support or refute our hypotheses and to make new observations. Students noticed melting features of the banks, such as more ice caves in snowbanks that directly faced the Sun and larger snowbanks in shaded areas.

Core Understandings

Often, when students are exposed to an authentic learning experience and are allowed to fully share their ideas, misconceptions rise to the surface. A few students thought that large snowbanks melt from the inside out. These students explained that at night the outer part of the snowbank freezes because of the cold air, forming a crust, but the inside continues to melt. One student was adamant that "the inside of a snowbank is all liquid." Many students at this age also think bulky coats and sweaters generate their own heat (Watson and Konicek 1990). They may transfer this idea to snowbanks.

The snow investigation provided the chance for students to observe water's phase changes firsthand. We took the students outside to examine the snowbanks around the schoolyard and to take core samples of the different layers. Using a 1 m long, clear plastic tube to take the core sample allowed students to see that the interior of a bank was ice throughout.

Back in the classroom, students pushed the core samples onto a tray and examined them carefully for texture and structure. Students saw evidence of *deposition* and *recrystallization* within the layers. Sand and salt that had been spread to clear roads appeared in the samples as dark layers in between lighter layers of snow, providing a visual record of deposition.

The snow from the core samples appeared very different from the fluffy flakes that fell during the storm: The core-sample snow had recrystallized into coarse, irregular, pea-sized grains. Students noted these findings in journal entries: Fresh snow is "fluffy and light," while snowbank snow, "looked like ice chunks; it looked like hail."

During the investigation, students also discussed their understandings of freezing and thawing. "When the water comes out of the snowbank, it freezes (at night) and turns into ice. Then day comes and turns it back into water. This keeps happening until the night isn't cold enough to freeze the water."

It was interesting that students assumed that the only way snow disappeared was through melting. They could not explain how salt-free snowdrifts shrank on below-freezing nights through *sublimation*—when water changes directly from ice to water vapor without melting. Students had not yet studied sublimation directly, but this topic would soon be covered in an upcoming unit exploring the phase changes of water and the states of matter. Examining the snowbank core samples laid a concrete foundation for that investigation.

Stories About Stratigraphy

We used the hands-on experience of examining snowbanks to promote literacy skills throughout this unit. For example, the vocabulary associated with the investigation was the foundation of students' spelling list for the week, and students recorded their thoughts in journals and completed reports to document their observations.

At each phase of instruction, students documented their thinking by writing about their snowbank experiences. Initially, students responded to specific prompts that directed their attention. As their knowledge base of snowbank formation grew, the nature of the writing assignments changed to more open-ended journaling and story creation.

In their writing, many students discussed the ages of the layers. For example, a student wrote, "After the first layer of snow, the snow comes again and leaves a layer on top." Another student wrote, "They have different colored layers, and the farther down, the older it is." This statement reflects emerging understanding of *superposition,* a key geologic concept.

Sample Study

The day after our outside snowbank observations, we passed around several layered sedimentary rock specimens. Students easily identified similarities between these and the snowbanks. Students quickly concluded that the layers in both the rock sample and in the snowbanks represent different episodes of deposition.

A thick layer of snow with a lot of sand, salt, and gravel thrown on top is evidence of the snowstorm that kept them home from school for three days. Other smaller layers represent shorter or less intense intervals of snowfall. Similarly, each layer in a sedimentary rock gives evidence of the conditions under which it formed. For example, strong currents are generally needed to move large pebbles, while silts and clays are deposited in quieter water.

A student explained the sequence of events in a snowbank: "Layers show what happens to the snowbank. First it snows, then the snowplows, road salt, or mud and dirt with rocks come to change the snowbank." Students were also able to correlate thick snow layers from photograph to photograph. It isn't the Grand Canyon, but in the 1–2 m tall snowbanks that line our streets for part of the winter, you daily see similar structures evolving on a smaller scale.

A Parfait Assessment

On the last day of the weeklong unit, we presented a final slide show of snowbanks interspersed with photos of sedimentary rock layers to help students take notice of their similar features and origins as an accumulation of falling particles. Much of the dialogue focused on how the varied layers of snowbanks reveal the history of local storms. Similarly, sedimentary rock layers show the sequence of deposition:

Figure 1.
Assessment rubric for description of snow bank model.

Criterion	Main Concept	Yes	No
Student states that the sequence of events for snowbank formation starts with the oldest, bottom layer.	Superposition	1	0
Vanilla pudding layers are described as representing snow accumulations.	Snowfall events	1	0
Crushed cookies or sprinkled candies are described as representing salt mixed with sand, clay, or gravel distributed by trucks and pushed on top of snowbank by plows or snowblower.	Plowing events	1	0
Student ascribes differences in snow layer thicknesses to amount of snowfall.	Layer thickness is related to snowfall	1	0
Student notes changes in the appearance of snow banks because of melting, refreezing, sublimation, or compaction.	Mechanisms for loss of snow volume	1	0
All writing is in complete sentences starting with a capital letter and ending with a period.		1	0
All spelling is correct.	Integration of writing skills	1	0
A diagram of the snowbank pudding model is included with parts labeled.		3	0
Total Points out of 10 Possible Points			

the history of floods, sandstorms, beach currents, mud slides, or other geologic processes that affected an area.

As a culminating activity, students created a model snowbank using vanilla pudding, crushed chocolate wafer cookies, peanut butter chips, and chocolate sprinkles. We took into account any student allergies before planning our food-related activity.

For assessment, we asked each student to draw a diagram of his or her model and write the story of the evolution of the "snowbank" that was created. The assessment rubric (Figure 1) focused on whether students could supply reasons for differences in layers (position, thickness, color, texture, and composition) in a snowbank and evaluated writing skills. Only after completing a suitable snowbank history and having it reviewed by a teacher could a student consume the snowbank pudding parfait.

Students enthusiastically built their models and described snowfalls, plow events, melting, more snow, and more episodes of sand and gravel distribution. One student who hadn't before excelled in science shared, "I never thought science could be so interesting, I want to do this again .... From now on I will always study snowbanks. I think they are awesome."

An In-School "Snow Day"

Students can perform investigations such as these even in places with limited snowfall. After a snowfall of only a few centimeters, students can make observations of the areas at which snow melts first. Or, an examination of snow footprints may prompt questions. Why do footprints often remain as icy silhouettes when the rest of the snow covering is gone? Are the footprints the same size as the shoes that created them?

And, without snow, be on the lookout for other local features, such as road cuts, that may present a similar opportunity. Finding authentic science experiences relevant to students' daily lives is an ongoing challenge. When snow totals aren't quite enough to cancel school, why not make an in-school "snow day"? Our students enjoyed their snow inquiry immensely. Yours will too.

Eric A. Olson is an assistant professor of childhood and adolescent science education, and Audrey C. Rule is a professor of childhood and early childhood education, both at the State University of New York (SUNY) at Oswego in Oswego, New York. Janet Dehm is a fourth-grade teacher at Kingsford Park School in Oswego, New York.

Resources

American Association for the Advancement of Science (AAAS). 1993. *Benchmarks for science literacy*. Washington, DC: Author.

National Research Council (NRC). 1996. *National Science Education Standards*. Washington, DC: National Academy Press.

Schmidt, P., J. S. Chadde, and M. Buenzli. 2003. Snowy entomology. *Science and Children* 41 (3): 40–45.

Watson, B., and R. Konicek. 1990. Teaching for conceptual change: Confronting children's experience. *Phi Delta Kappan* 7 (9): 680–685.

Connecting to the Standards
This article relates to the following National Science Education Standards (NRC 1996):

Content Standards
Grades K–4
Standard A: Science as Inquiry
• Abilities necessary to do scientific inquiry
Standard B: Physical Science
• Properties of objects and materials
Standard D: Earth and Space Science
• Properties of Earth materials
• Objects in the sky
• Changes in Earth and sky

Section 3

Beyond the School Day: Clubs and Expositions

Beyond the School Day

Clubs and Expositions

Teachers and students need more time. The day simply does not have enough contact time to cover all that students want and need to understand. But the time available after school can provide the resource needed to build on in-school learning. As we look at the skills needed in the 21st century, we consider the "soft skills" that will be in high demand. Communication, critical thinking, problem solving, creativity, innovation, collaboration: All are needed in any career students may pursue. Making use of the time available after school hours can help students develop an interest in science and, perhaps, an interest in science careers.

As a report from the Coalition for Science After School concluded:

After-school settings are optimal for providing engaging, hands-on STEM experiences, enabling students to apply, reinforce, and extend skills and concepts taught in school. And they are particularly conducive to project-based activities where a wide variety of children can participate in the design, construction, investigation, sense making, and communication of science projects. Furthermore, after school programs' connections to community organizations such as museums and science centers can change attitudes about math and science. Students from underrepresented communities can gain the necessary skills to compete in formal science classrooms. (2007)

After-school programs have proved to be effective supports for young people on a variety of fronts, including fostering healthy lifestyles, preventing dropouts, boosting students' academic achievement and self-esteem, and helping young people find and develop their passions (Hart 2006). As the public and parents become more concerned about today's students falling behind in math and science, they are realizing that the extra hours after school can be used to help our young people keep up and even excel. In fact, a recent poll found that 81% of Americans favor expanding after-school programs as a way to increase students' access to math and science education, even if this increases the per-pupil spending. Those of us who have conducted science fairs know that it is not possible to provide the type and amount of support needed by students within the regular hours of the school day and still teach everything in the curriculum. Students need help, and we don't want all of that extra help being provided at home. Volunteers can be instructed in how to provide the kind of support students require after school hours and fill that need.

Rethink the term *science fair*. The vision of parents creating the projects, competitions among students, and only prize winners feeling a sense of accomplishment are no longer part of the science expositions today.

Clubs and summer camps provide opportunities for students to participate in activities they have selected themselves. There is help for those creating this type of experience for children. The Coalition for Science After School offers a blueprint including a rationale, and exemplary program models. Many informal science centers provide traveling science explorations. They will bring activities, living organisms, and challenges to a club or camp. Visit the website of your local zoo, museum, or science center to determine if they have these resources available. There are also for-profit agencies now offering science explorations that may become a part of club activities.

In This Section *(articles are in italics)*

Evaluating science projects at the time of the science fair is too late. Students should be provided with the tools to conduct self-evaluations and create their project based on guided criteria. *What Makes for a Good Science Fair Project?* goes beyond the surface of the slick look of some projects and considers the vital components of a project that allow students to do what scientists do rather than following "the" scientific method. Projects are judged on process rather than results.

Many teachers are concerned about the quality of projects selected by students for science fairs. *Four Tools for Science Fair Success* concentrates on providing guidance in helping students conduct true inquiry-based research projects. Tips and teacher-tested strategies include selecting a topic; setting a timeline with checkpoints; considering safety, adherence to rules, and appropriate supervision for experiments; revision of projects for continual improvement; and running after-school project clinics.

A Revamped Science Expo describes what is involved in requiring a project based on state science frameworks with the goal of guiding students away from cookbook experiments. The Science Expo becomes a night when students and the community come together to share and learn about science inquiry, processes, and habits of mind. This Expo is clearly not a competition. A step-by-step process for establishing a testable question is one of the main keys to the success of these projects. Not until questions are established are guidelines for creating a project, exposition etiquette, and set-up instructions provided to participants.

By describing how to take advantage of after-school time to provide more science opportunities, *Extending Science Learning Through Science Clubs* provides a model for establishing a science club. Concrete steps in how to set the tone for the club with teachers serving as advisers and students as officers, activity suggestions, fund raising, project ideas, and the rewards gained from club participation are a part of the overview.

Bitten by the Science Bug describes a primary summer science camp. It provides evidence that children are never too young to participate in this type of activity. Designing this camp was ground breaking for the school system. Taking preK–K students seriously as science investigators was the goal—the team outlines all of the logistics to accomplish that goal and much more.

Another group of young scientists with special needs are girls. An overnight weekend summer science camp, *Girls in Science Rule!*, was created to encourage girls who want to learn more about science. Topics from safety in the wilderness to insect study engage the girls throughout the weekend. Pre- and postsurveys of the girls indicate positive growth in attitudes toward science and increased self-confidence.

References

Coalition for After School Science. 2006. After school programs: at the STEM of learning

Issue brief No. 26. *www.afterschoolalliance.org/ issue_briefs/issue_STEM_26.pdf*

Hart, P. D. 2006. *Keeping our edge: Americans speak on education and competitiveness.* Poll conducted for ETS.

National Science Teachers Association. 1999. NSTA position statement: Science competitions. *www.nsta.org/about/positions.aspx.*

Partnership for 21st Century Skills. 2007. *www.21stcenturyskills.org.*

Resources

The articles listed are available through the Learning Center on the NSTA web site at *http:// learningcenter.nsta.org.*

After school training kit. National Partnership for Afterschool Learning. *www.sedl.org/afterschool.*

Eick, C., M. L. Ewald, E. Kling, and C. Shaw. 2005. Reaching out to outreach. *Science Scope* 28: 36–37.

Flynn, E. 2007. The Philbrick Science Showcase. *Science and Children.* 45: 41–44.

Gore, S. 2006. Engineering-a-future for tomorrow's young women. *Science Scope* 31: 46-48.

LeDee, O., A. Mosser, T. Gamble, G. Childs, and K. Oberhauser. 2007. A science club takes action. *Science and Children* 45: 35–37.

Moore, N. 2006. Rocket boys and girls. *Science Scope* 31: 54–55.

Parker, V., and B. Gerber. 2000. Science festival fun: A teaching and learning experience. *Science Scope* 23: 16–19.

Coalition for Science After School. 2007. Science in after school: blueprint for action. *http:// qt.exploratorium.edu/csas/resources.html.*

National Science Teachers Association (NSTA). *Science fairs plus: reinventing an old favorite.* 2003. Arlington, VA: NSTA Press.

Torres, A., and D. Vittti. 2007. A kinder-science fair. *Science and Children* 45: 21–25.

Tubbs, J. 2007. Take the science fair online! *Science and Children* 45: 45–49.

What Makes for a Good Science Fair Project?

By Bill Robertson

Ah, one of my pet peeves. I used to judge a lot of science fairs, but I stopped because I seldom agreed with the evaluations of the other judges. Our main point of disagreement usually centered on glitz versus substance. No doubt about it—a science fair project that looks impressive tends to sway the judges. Of course, I had other disagreements with other judges, so I'm glad for the opportunity to suggest what people should look for in judging science fairs, and thus what students should focus on in doing the projects. My main concerns are with the kinds of questions the project answers and the extent to which the project mimics what scientists actually do in an investigation.

Choosing the Right Question

One way to address this issue is to name a few questions that are *not* good for science fair projects. "Why is the sky blue?" "Can plants survive without water?" and "What causes volcanoes?" are examples of questions that aren't so great. The reason they're not great is that scientists already know the answers to those questions. A student doing a project inspired by such questions is simply learning a concept and reporting on it. Now, that's okay for a science classroom. It's good to learn answers to those questions, and students can use inquiry to answer those questions. The purpose of a science fair, though, should be for students to answer a question, the answer to which cannot be found in a textbook. Here are a few questions for which you won't find textbook answers and which might be pretty interesting for students to answer:

- Does chewing gum help students do better in school?
- Does playing video games improve your reactions and your memory?
- Do people in certain-colored cars obey traffic laws better?

These happen to be actual science fair questions I've come across over the years. The students who posed the questions had various reasons for asking the questions, but the important thing was that the students genuinely wanted to know the answers to these questions. Clearly, finding out that chewing gum helps you do better in class or discovering that playing video games is good for you are pieces of information useful for the average student. Beyond that, though, the questions lend themselves to true investigation.

Do What Scientists Do Rather Than Follow the "Scientific Method"

In the heading for this section, the words *scientific method* are in quotes because there are disagreements as to what constitutes the scientific method. There is a "textbook" definition, though, that goes something like the following:

- ask a question
- do background research
- construct a hypothesis
- test your hypothesis by doing an experiment
- analyze your data and draw a conclusion
- communicate your results

Anyone who has done basic research in any scientific discipline can tell you that scientists only rarely follow this kind of structured approach. Although scientists might begin with a general question, this is followed by a whole bunch of messing around with things to become familiar with the territory. This messing around leads to refinement or even restructuring of the original question, and it might lead to a totally new question. Let me give you an example from my own research and then an example of how this might apply to a science fair project.

When I began graduate work in science education and cognitive science, I wanted to study the difference between people who understand science and people who memorize science. From my experience I knew there was a difference, but I had only primitive ideas of how to determine the difference. It took me a year and a half to get to where I knew how to conduct

my research. Part of that was spent researching what others had done, part was spent simply talking to physics students, and part was spent talking to physics professors. My adviser gave me great advice in the beginning, which was to define *understanding* and *memorization* for myself before researching what others had done. That helped me keep my own perspective on the issue rather than simply parrot what other researchers thought. So, I did a lot of messing around before I formulated any kind of researchable question. The bottom line was that I didn't formulate a hypothesis and then jump into my experiments.

Let's apply that to the chewing-gum question. To approach this as a scientist might, one should spend a fair amount of time observing other students and talking to teachers in an effort to define what one means by "doing better in school." Do you look at test scores alone? Does attentiveness in class count? There are lots of ways of determining how well one does in school, and you have to refine things down to a specific measure of performance in order to get meaningful results. You also should simply observe students chewing and not chewing gum in a variety of school situations (gotta find a sympathetic teacher to allow you to do this one!). In the process, you might find behaviors related to chewing gum in class that have nothing to do with your original question. For example, you might discover that kids who chew gum in class tend to talk less. How does that relate to performance, or does it relate to performance at all?

Controlling Variables

One of the most difficult things for students to do is figure out how to structure an investigation so as to focus on the question they're asking while minimizing the effect of other factors. For chewing gum in class, you want to be able to control such contributing factors as the time of day, the day of the week, the style of the teacher, the health of the students, and the prior performance of the students. Suppose you are going to measure performance with before and after tests. It would be a good idea to give students various kinds of tests without gum chewing involved at all, so you know something about how much students either improve or don't improve based on things other than gum chewing. In other words, you have to mess around with things again before settling on a procedure. A student who does a good job of messing around and has seriously addressed the issue of controlling variables should be commended for a job well done, even if it means not "finishing" the project with a distinct conclusion.

Sometimes You Discover Nothing

Often scientists learn nothing from an experiment other than how to restructure the experiment. Neat, clean results are the exception rather than the rule. Yet, I have seen many science fair judges mark students down for not getting those neat, clean results. It's okay to learn nothing from an experiment other than what you did wrong, because that's a common result in science. This is especially true given the relatively short amount of time students have for a science fair project. If scientists can go years without a decisive answer to a question, why expect students to get that decisive answer in a month or two?

Judge the Process More Than the Result

Given the short amount of time students have to complete a project, given that questions that truly interest the student are likely to be complicated and difficult to define, and given that true scientific investigation seldom follows the structured steps outlined in the typical expression of the scientific method, it makes sense to grade students with a greater emphasis on the process of the investigation than on an eye-catching, snazzy finished product. In this way, the students gain a better understanding

of scientific investigation and learn to focus on what scientists do rather than on how much mom and dad can help them create a cool-looking report.

I should end by saying that, over the years, I have seen improvement in what schools require in a science fair project. It is more and more common to find requirements that the students do an experiment rather than a report. That said, there is still too much reliance on the structured scientific method and not enough focus on, or understanding of, what scientists really do. Needless to say, the judges one uses for a science fair have at least as much influence on what the students get out of the experience as do the requirements outlined by the school.

Bill Robertson is the author of the NSTA Press book series, Stop Faking It! Finally Understanding Science So You Can Teach It.

Four Tools for Science Fair Success

By Sherry Weaver Smith, Barbara Messmer, Bill Storm, and Cheryl Weaver

Have you been reluctant to take on running a science fair? Perhaps you fear a fair comprising of slapdash, last-minute projects. You likely feel pressure to teach to the standards. We are a team of veteran teachers who have overcome these same concerns by creating and testing several ways to improve the science fair experience in our classrooms. We have added to our programs by using the resources of Science Buddies, a nonprofit organization dedicated to providing free science fair project ideas, answers, and tools for teachers and students in grades K–12 (see Internet Resources).

We offer four ideas to guide students in creating true inquiry-based projects as they accomplish some steps independently at home. Two of our ideas, the Topic Selection Wizard and Science Project Timeline, are appropriate for all science fair programs, even new ones. For existing programs, the Black Box of Project Improvement and After-School Project Clinic improve project quality and broaden participation.

Topic Selection Wizard

Key objective: Help students find topics of their own interest.

In classrooms across the country, students have used the Science Buddies online Topic Selection Wizard to find their own science project area of interest (see Internet Resources). In our classrooms, when students found project ideas related to their own areas of interest, they became more committed to working on their projects long term. In addition, using knowledge they already had, they were able to come up with predictions and ideas for experimental procedures more quickly and accurately.

The Topic Selection Wizard is a tool that not only helps uncover interests but also leads students to science project questions that are inquiry based and practical. The Wizard covers six major science categories and 25 specific interest areas, a wide range that has something for every child. At Crestmont Elementary in Roseville, California, coauthor Barbara Messmer's fifth-grade students used the Wizard during weekly computer lab time in preparation for a science fair. First, children took the Science Interest Survey, which they completed in an average of 10 minutes. The survey included 36 fun questions such as, "Are you interested in science fiction stories involving faster-than-light travel and 'beams' that do amazing things?" Then the Wizard presented each student with a custom-tailored list of suitable project ideas, complete with a key illustrating such aspects as difficulty level and safety, which each student reviewed for approximately 30 minutes.

There were two main results. First, 85% of the students found the core idea for their project using the Wizard. They successfully overcame the trickiest part of the science fair journey: starting out with a testable question. The other 15% of students felt committed to other topics that they discovered through interactions with family members or other experiences in their lives. Teachers had to work more diligently with these children to convert their interest areas into testable project idea questions.

Second, the children who used the website were passionate about their projects. Four of five children interviewed were excited to carry on with the same topics in the next fair.

Science Project Timeline

Key objective: Require work over the long term and assess project progress at key checkpoints along the way.

In our schools, teachers guided children's science projects in class by assessing progress at key checkpoints. Figure 1 is a synthesis of the schedules that they used and the one suggested by Science Buddies online.

This strategy reduced the two project extremes: parent-generated masterpieces and slapdash night-before trifles. Overall, the timeline broke long-term science projects into manageable pieces. Teachers reviewed work at each step, so that students who were off track could start going in the right direction without wasting effort. For example, the timeline set an

early deadline for students to develop a testable question. Teachers signed off on this key task early on, so that students could begin experimentation safely and with confidence that their experiments would relate to their questions.

As you are considering these checkpoints to teach the students, always keep project safety as your primary objective. Assess safety when children decide on questions, when they write their experimental procedures, and when they bring display boards to the fair.

Science Buddies recommends that teachers evaluate a student's project against three tests of safety:

- Is it safe for other people or animals that are involved?
- If the student is going to another science fair after your own, does it meet the rules for that fair?
- Finally, has the student addressed all other safety concerns to your satisfaction? Make students themselves address safety issues in their project proposal. Then you should evaluate:
  - Where will the experiment be performed?
  - What safety gear will be used?
  - Who will be supervising the experiment? Do they have common sense and/or training in the procedures being used?

The Science Buddies web site has additional information about safety, including more detail on the previous suggestions, as well as guidelines for some special areas such as chemistry, microbiology, and rocketry.

The Black Box of Project Improvement

Key objective: Develop a system that encourages students to continually improve and revise their projects according to provided rubrics.

Crestmont Elementary fifth-grade students

Figure 1.
Science fair project timeline, from *www.sciencebuddies.org*.

Assignment	To Do or Read (Readings are in the Project Guide at *www.sciencebuddies.org*)	Hand In (Worksheets are on the Teachers Resources page at *www.sciencebuddies.org*)	Duration	Due Date
Ask a question	Complete the Topic Selection Wizard (*www.sciencebuddies.org*). Read "The Scientific Method." Read "Your Question."	Print the Topic Selection Wizard results for your teacher, or write down your project question. Fill in your Project Proposal Form.	2 weeks	
Do background research Part I: Collect information	Read "Background Research Plan." Read "Finding Information." Read "Bibliography."	Complete the Background Research Plan Worksheet. Complete the Bibliography Worksheet.	1 week	
Do background research Part II: Write your research paper	Read "Research Paper."	Write your research paper. Complete the Research Paper Checklist.	1 week	
Construct a hypothesis	Read "Variables for Beginners." Read "Hypothesis."	Complete the Variables and Hypothesis Worksheet.	1 week	
Test your hypothesis by doing an experiment Part I: Design an experimental procedure	Read "Experimental Procedure." Read "Materials List."	Write a materials list, including measurements. Write experimental procedure steps.	1 week	
Test your hypothesis by doing an experiment Part II: Do an experiment	Read "Conducting an Experiment." Repeat your experiment at least three times.	Write one paragraph describing your observations. Bring in the data that you collected in a data table.	2 weeks	
Analyze your data and draw a conclusion	Read "Data Analysis and Graphs." Read "Conclusions."	Make at least one graph. Write your conclusion.	1 week	
Communicate your results	Read "Display Board." Make the pieces of your display board: title, question, hypothesis, materials list, experimental procedure, data analysis, conclusions, and acknowledgements.	Display Board pieces, not yet attached to the board.	1 week	
Congratulations! It's time for the Science Fair			Total: 10 weeks	

Do you need to customize this timeline? download it on the Teacher Resources Page at *www.sciencebuddies.com*.

Figure 2.
Black Box science project grading rubric.

Name_____

Date _____

Science Fair Background Research Paper Grade Sheet

Title	/5
Introduction	/5
At Least Three Supported Paragraphs	/10
Conclusion	/5
Important Terms Defined	/10
Research Questions Answered	/10
Can Make Predictions from Research	/10
Relevant Math Plan for Data Explained	/5
All Sources Referenced Properly (MLA Format)	/10
At Least Three References (Not Just Web Sources)	/5
Alphabetized Bibliography	/5
Spelling	/5
Grammar and Punctuation	/5
Neatness	/5
Punctuality	/5
Style Deduction _____	/100

Points will be deducted from the total score if the wording of this report is not in the student's own writing style.

Source: Crestmont Elementary, Roseville, California, Barbara Messmer

The chance for improvement modeled the scientific process in the real world, where projects are never fully done and graded—and there are opportunities to loop back and improve.

The Black Box approach took place at two key phases during the projects: when students were researching and writing the background research paper (review of literature), and when students were compiling their final science fair project reports. The background research paper phase began in the second week of the two-month project, after students created a testable question, and it ended in the fourth week. All students turned in their first draft on a set due date. Then the teacher conducted the first round of project improvement by reviewing each draft using a score sheet (Figure 2) over a one- or two-day period. The teacher photocopied each draft and score sheet to document improvements in the student's file folder.

Students then decided whether to improve their scores. Guided by teacher comments and where they were missing points, students did revisions in one or two days, and then the teacher repeated the steps above for each student submitting corrections. Students chose how many times they wanted to submit improvements and the target points that they wanted to earn. Students were accountable for their own results.

The next phase of project improvement occurred one week before the fair. Students brought in all of the sections of their final report. In this phase, the teacher completed a checklist of all of the different report sections, such as materials list and conclusion. Students provided missing items or fixed deficient items quickly, over one or two days, as most had their documents on computers. Although most students completed revisions in the one week between turning

followed a timeline with a twist. They turned in assignments according to a timeline, but they also had the chance to redo key steps to improve their projects and grades at several points along the way. Their teacher encouraged them to keep improving their background research papers and final reports, and she kept a record of all of the drafts in a file box called the "Black Box."

in their final reports and attending the science fair, some students even had the chance to make further improvements after the fair.

A case study of how students improved their background research papers early in the process illustrates the effectiveness of the Black Box. Students fell into three groups. One group of students primarily made mechanical errors in grammar and spelling. These students often failed to create the single most overlooked item of first drafts: a "math plan" for data analysis. For example, a math plan should indicate:

- What the student will measure
- How he or she will measure it
- That he or she will record measurements in a data table
- The number of trials planned
- What he or she will calculate, such as the mean of all of the measurements

In the second, most typical group, students persevered through up to three attempts at their reports over a one-month period. In a first draft, one student within this group had conducted detailed research on his topic: the effect of temperature on the bouncing of tennis balls. He had not made the leap to connect his research to an actionable experiment. The teacher determined that, although the student had done research on what makes balls bounce, he did not have an understanding of how to design an experimental procedure to test this.

Through the process, in second and third drafts, this student grounded his experimental procedure in research. After discovering that temperature would probably have an effect on bouncing, he wrote a paragraph about how he would heat and cool the tennis balls and how he would drop them from a consistent, controlled height. When planning data analysis, he decided to measure bounce height in a reliable way by creating a measuring board with lines. He set a goal to compare the data from three trials and calculate a mean. In a third draft, he perfected

his writing and source citations. In the end, he improved his score by two letter grades, but more important, he learned to persevere to understand a topic.

In the third group, a small number of students had to revise their work significantly. These students had trouble picking questions that they could answer through investigation. They could not conceptualize how the data they were gathering would lead them to conclusions. After Black Box checkpoints, all were able to start with new topics and succeed in their second tries.

Apart from giving the students a structure to improve, Black Box records established to outside judges that the students did their own work. Serving as an additional assessment, all five fifth graders who went on to the district fair received medals. Two of the five fourth graders received medals. Going forward, teachers plan to refine the Black Box process by putting more emphasis on children's initial experimental procedures so that they ensure early on that their experiments are practical and doable.

After-School Project Clinic

Key objective: Level the playing field for children who do not have access to knowledgeable mentors.

At Valley Oak Elementary in Davis, California, children had a chance to reach their investigative potential by attending an after-school science project clinic. Science specialists Bill Storm and Sarita Cooper provided a diverse group of fourth- through sixth-grade students, most with socioeconomic disadvantages, with the extra support and mentoring needed to create and present successful inquiry projects at the mandatory science fair in their district.

In the first step, teachers approached the local university, University of California, Davis, to find student volunteers, including education students seeking internships as well as independent students seeking community service. Approximately 20 volunteers signed up to help these students. Before any volunteer recruitment and management effort, familiarize yourself with the safety rules, such as the need for background checks or supervision, of your school and district.

The second step was to find students requiring additional support. The science teachers polled all staff to gain insight as to students who needed academic or language support; required sponsorship for materials, including a display board; lacked support at home; or resided in group homes.

Counselors, English language teachers, classroom staff, resource teachers, psychologists, and speech therapists all worked to identify students in these categories. Science teachers also informed students that extra support was available, and a few additional students beyond those identified by staff came forward to participate. The science teachers then asked for parental permission for the students to participate. In the end, around 30 students needed extra support out of a population of 360 students in the upper-elementary grades.

In the third step, science teachers provided structure for the enthusiastic university volunteers and students to work on their projects. For six weeks they worked one-on-one with elementary school students on Wednesday afternoons at the school. The mere presence of special people from the university encouraged students to participate in the after-school time. Volunteers used a six-week timeline of assignments and expectations to guide the students.

After students picked a question, the volunteers accompanied the students into the library to do research and to the computer lab to type elements of the project. Students and volunteers together especially enjoyed "shopping" for project materials in the school's two science labs.

Throughout the process, volunteers and students benefited from school resources, such as a Spanish translation on the school web site of all informational materials available, which included a letter to parents introducing the science fair, an assignment timeline, topic selection homework, a permission/sponsor form, a grading checklist, and project ideas.

The culmination came when the volunteers helped the students create their display boards, a task for which the program provided appropriate latitude. For example, some students presented display boards in their native language.

The main result of the program was that the volunteers helped students meet a key objective to gain public acknowledgement of personal work. At the fair, students had the chance to show their projects to the volunteers and their families. They saw for themselves that their work mattered to a larger community. These successes were the results of an entire school team getting involved in the science fair process, including resource teachers, paraeducator aides, English language teachers, after-school homework teachers, and volunteers.

Pick One, and Get Going!

The ideas you choose to implement at your science fair depend upon the issues that are most salient at your school. For example, if your key issue is students needing basic resources to participate, then the After-School Project Clinic may be the most appropriate idea for you. If you are just starting a program, however, you might want to start with the Topic Selection Wizard and Science Project Timeline. Add the Black Box, the idea of improving continually when you have a year or two of experience. However and whatever you implement, there are resources available every step of the way to help you make the science fair at your school the valuable inquiry experience it can be.

Sherry Weaver Smith is a writer for Science Buddies, a nonprofit organization, based in California. Barbara Messmer teaches a fifth-grade Gifted and Talented Education (GATE) class at Crestmont Elementary School in Roseville, California. Bill Storm is a science specialist for grades five and six at

Valley Oak Elementary School in Davis, California. Cheryl Weaver is an educational consultant and retired elementary school teacher.

Resources

Fredericks, A. D., and I. Asimov. 2001. *Science fair handbook: The complete guide for teachers and parents.* Tucson, AZ: Good Year Books.

National Research Council (NRC). 1996. *National Science Education Standards.* Washington, DC: National Academy Press.

Internet
Science Buddies
www.sciencebuddies.org

Connecting to the Standards

This article relates to the following National Science Education Standards (NRC 1996).

Science Teaching Standards

Standard A: Teachers of science plan an inquiry-based science program for their students.

Standard B: Teachers of science guide and facilitate learning.

Standard C: Teachers of science engage in ongoing assessment of their teaching and of student learning.

Standard D: Teachers of science design and manage learning environments that provide students with the time, space, and resources needed for learning science.

Standard E: Teachers of science develop communities of science learners that reflect the intellectual rigor of scientific inquiry and the attitudes and social values conducive to science learning.

Content Standards
Grades K–8
Standard A: Science as Inquiry
- Abilities necessary to do scientific inquiry
- Understanding about scientific inquiry

A Revamped Science Expo

By Lorna Barth

At the elementary school level, science fairs are often social events, complete with hired "science" entertainments, hands-on activities, and family fun. Although science festivals like this can be great for promoting positive attitudes toward science, they don't always reflect meaningful science learning.

The vision at our school was to take our science fair event and turn it into an experience that gave meaning and purpose to science learning. We redesigned our science fair to meet state standards and made it a required assignment for the fourth- through sixth-grade levels. The goal was to guide students away from cookbook experiments toward developing a question about their environment into a testable and measurable experiment. The revamped "Science Expo" became a night for students to show each other and the community what they've learned about science inquiry, processes, and habits of mind.

It's Their Project

The one nonnegotiable aspect of the Expo project was that students had to choose their topic and question on their own. No one can come up with an awesome experiment like a 10-year-old kid. The Expo projects gave teachers (and parents) a chance to see what their students found fascinating enough to spend time investigating and how students thought as they approached ways to test, change, measure, document, and write about their investigation. The project wasn't designed to test students' abilities to follow step-by-step directions of an existing experiment; it was designed to view what students could do when given the freedom to explore their own questions in a safe and structured scientific manner. It was a way for teachers to see if the curriculum itself was doing what it is designed to do: teach the processes of science.

In February, eight weeks before the scheduled date of the Expo, I introduced the project to students. This was a gentle heads-up introduction, just to get students thinking about the Expo and to let them know that project materials—such as display boards, project requirements, and rubric—would be handed out in two weeks. I told the students in the fifth- and sixth-grade classes that each student would be creating a project as part of his or her inquiry grade in science class and presenting it at the Expo. (Students in the fourth grade could work with a partner, but fifth and sixth graders were to complete individual investigations.) The main goal was for students to come up with a question they were interested in and then turn that question into a testable and measurable investigation. Students could choose any topic, as long as the question was testable and could be investigated in their own environment.

Questions, Questions

Once the setup was established, we turned our attention to discussing how to turn a question into a testable and measurable investigation. Students quickly began sharing project ideas that popped into their heads. Whenever a student proposed

an idea, I asked two questions: "How can you test that?" and "How are you going to measure it?" These questions helped students consider the parameters of their idea and determine whether it would be possible to investigate the question within the limits of our time and resources.

Once students got past the idea of what a science fair–type project "had" to be, they delved into their own environment, and the possibilities really opened up. For example, students started asking questions such as "Do different types of candles burn hotter?" and "Are brown eggshells harder than white eggshells?," which could be developed into investigations for the Expo. (See Figure 1 for a list of additional questions that were presented at the Expo.)

In our introductory discussions, we talked about finding the one thing that was the part of their question to test. Students' investigations should have only one measurement to make for their measurements to be true and the collection of data easy to track. Trickier questions usually received repeated mantras of "How are you going to test that?" and "How are you going to measure that?" before students could pare down to a workable idea. For example, two fourth-grade students suggested, "We want to find out if the lack of sleep will cause problems."

I asked them, "How are you going to test that?" The girls looked at each other, conferred for a few moments, and replied, "One of us will stay up all night and then play soccer the next day and see if there is a difference."

"But how are you going to measure that?" I asked. "She could just be having an off day."

My question led to another miniconference, this time a little longer and more animated.

Next, students suggested, "We decided to both stay up all night and do the same puzzle and see if there is a difference."

Again I gently asked, "How are you going to measure it in order to collect data?" and they quickly said, "Oh, we're going to use a timer and see how long it takes us to do it each time."

This was a typical exchange as students honed

Figure 1.
Student-developed questions.

- What is the effect of cola on teeth?
- Will your core body temperature rise when you eat spicy food?
- Does sight affect opinion of taste?
- Does vinegar affect the bounce of a boiled egg?
- Do different kinds of music affect the growth of plants?
- Which egg has the hardest shell: brown or white?
- Which toothpaste whitens best on eggshells boiled in coffee?
- What type of cookie sheet cooks chocolate chip cookies the fastest?
- What is the effect of temperature on magnetism?
- Will sleep deprivation affect puzzle-making skills?
- Does petroleum jelly affect the drag on swim fins?
- How does fat content affect the rate of chocolate ice cream melting?
- Can biomass (cow manure) generate electricity?

project ideas. In less than 10 minutes these students had turned a big, loose question into a specific and measurable investigation. It took about one class period for students to understand the idea of a testable question. Most students left school that day with an idea of what they wanted to investigate and needed only short follow-up consultations with me by e-mail or at my desk. I looked at each student's proposed question to see if there was an understanding of the project, and if it appeared to be on the right track I gave the question the go-ahead.

Completing the Projects

During the course of the next two weeks, all of the students had established a testable question and investigation to work on. Then I provided students with materials packets that spelled out the project requirements, including the template for the display board format, information for parents and students about the rules of parental involvement in the project, and the grading rubric that would be used to evaluate the projects.

No class time was used to complete the Expo projects—the investigations were carried out at home. Because our school required participation in the science fair for all students in grades five and six, the parent-teacher organization generously purchased the display boards for the projects. (Younger students were furnished boards if they presented a testable question and presented their investigations as nongraded participants in the Expo.) Supplying the display boards ensured that all students had what they needed. I reiterated that the project focus was the investigation, not the display board. I told my kids, "You do not go to a football game to look at the field, you go to a game to see the game that is played on that field."

Students were required to plan and devise a way to test and measure their question themselves, so they needed to provide any supplies needed for the investigation. As part of their display, students had to list the investigation's required materials, procedures, and safety requirements. This enabled teachers to assess the procedural thinking of students as opposed to their abilities to follow directions to put together a project.

Students had six weeks to put together their projects. Four weeks prior to the Expo, I introduced the rubrics for each grade level. We went over the rubrics in class, and I told students they could bring me any part of their project for consultation, but class time would not be used for Expo projects. The only exception I made was for the students in the special education class, who completed their project ("Do Worms Like Pencil Shavings in Their Environment?") as a group during the school day using the class Worm Bin. The class was very proud to share its display board on the Expo night alongside all the other students' work.

Exposition Etiquette and Setup

The day before the Expo, I visited the fourth-through sixth-grade classrooms to discuss exposition etiquette, answer questions, and provide support. I showed the students a sample board and then modeled how to stand, how to respond to project questions, and how to thank the people who listened to their presentations. I emphasized that the general atmosphere for the evening was more like a piano recital—with regard to respect and attention one pays to participants—than a carnival experience.

The next morning, we set up the gym as if it were a science conference, with all student projects on display. Tables were aligned in rows by teacher's name and in the area for that grade level. Tables around the perimeter of the gym were for fourth-grade projects. The center of the gym was lined with rows of tables with a center aisle down the middle. These tables held fifth- and sixth-grade projects. The requirements stated that any investigation apparatus could take up only the space on the table in front of the tri-fold display board—larger designs had to be represented by models or by photographs in a binder in front of the display board.

After the boards were set up, teachers from the primary grades took their classes into the gym for a "private showing" before the evening event. It was exciting to watch the older students explain their investigations to younger scientists. It was also a valuable opportunity to practice presenting their projects and following the logistical plan of the evening. (At our event, each grade level has only a limited number of students on the floor with their presentations at one time. Presenters are called in alphabetical order in 10-minute intervals, at which point students move to their project board, put on their lab coat, and begin their presentation.)

The Big Night

On Expo night, excitement was in the air. Before presentations began, students proudly examined their displays—and graded their own work. To do this, students looked at their finished project and reviewed each element on the rubric glued to the back of the board. Parents and students were required to sign the rubric after the self-grade, which encouraged personal responsibility for academic performance.

The presenting students wore lab coats, making them easily identifiable as they stood beside their projects and answered questions about their investigations. With enthusiasm and poise students shared their scientific findings to the gym filled with peers, adults, parents, teachers, and administrators. We noticed many younger students and siblings engaged with older students and asking questions about the projects, providing the presenters with an excellent chance to be mentors.

After the event, the boards were returned to students' classroom teachers for evaluation. Teachers scored their own classroom projects because they knew their students best. With the help of a few audience volunteers, dismantling the Expo was a simple task. Because all the students used the same kind of display boards and there were no elaborate displays or models to dismantle,

moving the projects to the classrooms was accomplished in less than 15 minutes.

Authentic Learning

Traditionally, science fairs have been viewed as competitions for scientifically inclined students. By changing the venue from festival to a required academic *exposition* and by providing detailed student requirements for project completion, the emphasis moved from cookbook projects to authentic investigations built upon questions generated by the students themselves, ensuring a focus on inquiry for all.

Lorna Barth developed the Science Expo while teaching as a science specialist at Sunrise Elementary School in Redmond, Washington, and now teaches at Tolt Middle School in Carnation, Washington.

Acknowledgments

Thanks to Science Methods Instructor Carol Kubota at the University of Washington, Bothell, for her guidance and support, and the Tolt Middle School Science Team—Ruth Cruz, Charlene Short, Kathy Buck, Theresa O'Shea and Carol Hall—for their advice and mentorship.

Resources

National Research Council (NRC). 1996. *National Science Education Standards*. Washington, DC: National Academy Press.

Saul, W., D. Dieckman, C. Pearce, and D. Neutze. 2005. *Beyond the science fair: Creating a kids' inquiry conference*. Portsmouth, NH: Heinemann.

Connecting to the Standards
This article relates to the following *National Science Education Standards* (NRC 1996).

Science Teaching Standards
Standard F:
Teachers of science actively participate in the ongoing planning and development of the school science program.

Extending Science Learning Through Science Clubs

By Karen Mesmer

Is 50 minutes of classroom instruction not enough time to satisfy your students' desire to learn science? Establishing a science club may be just the solution. Five years ago, I helped organize a middle level science club to extend science learning for our students.

The science club does not replace the science curriculum but rather supplements and enhances the learning experience. Although club events may not always coincide with what students are learning in the classroom, they do allow students to explore specific science topics in greater depth. Club activities are also designed to encourage parental participation. We generally have five or so parents attend our Friday night or Saturday activities.

Membership is open to all students who fill out an application explaining why they would like to be in the science club. In addition to the application, students must also complete a survey to identify their interests, which range from aviation to zoology. We then try to plan club activities around the students' interests.

Students meet twice a month, either after school or on Saturdays, depending on the activity. We try to coordinate club activites to avoid conflicts with other extracurricular school events, but sometimes they can't be avoided. Students are permitted unlimited excused absences, but are limited to three unexcused absences per school year. If a student has more than three unexcused absences in a year, he or she is removed from the club.

Each October, we have an election of club officers. Students running for office give a speech, and club members vote by secret ballot. Any member can run for office as long as he or she has been in the science club for more than one year. Once elected, officers assist the club advisors with many tasks, s uch as planning club activities, organizing fund-raisers, introducing guest speakers at club events, and compiling the science club scrapbook. In addition to two club advisers, we have many parent and teacher volunteers who help throughout the year. Our school district provides funding for travel and teacher reimbursement, and club members raise extra money by selling T-shirts and sponsoring a dance.

Past activities include going on field trips, listening to guest speakers, and working cooperatively on science-related projects. Students have visited zoos; aquariums; museums; university research labs; science-related companies, such as soil and water analysis labs and an aviation design company; wildlife centers; state parks; and nature preserves. Students are required to turn in signed permission slips before attending any of the field trips. We also review all safety issues that pertain to each activity.

Guest speakers have presented on preserving crane habitats, rehabilitating injured wildlife, and using biotechnology in our everyday lives. I recommend you check with your local speaker's bureau and local environmental organizations to find speakers who are appropriate. Previous science club projects have included collecting prairie seeds to restore wildlife; raising money to "adopt" a wolf pack, humpback whale, manatee, whooping crane, and a rain forest; conducting chemical and biotic analysis of nearby water sources; and participating in the State Science Olympiad competition.

Our science club has generated tremendous enthusiasm for science, both in and out of school. It is now one of the largest clubs in the school and boasts a diverse group of more than 70 students. In fact, our numbers have grown so large that we are now forming a separate seventh-grade club and a joint eighth-and-ninth-grade club.

Because of their club experiences, many students are now exploring careers in science. For example, one student has decided to become a forensic scientist because of his visit to the anatomy and physiology labs at the local university. Another student is interning at a biotechnology company, and still another recently attended a four-week summer marine biology institute. Even students who might not choose a science-related career see that science can be enjoyable. Students of all abilities and backgrounds now realize that science is both rewarding and fun.

One of my favorite club activities was a visit to the International Crane Foundation in Baraboo. Students learned about the foundation's captive breeding program and preservation efforts while observing 15 different types of cranes. Students also learned how to use radio-tracking equipment used by ornithologists. The foundation allowed our club to visit free of charge as long as club members helped to pick prairie seeds for the prairie restoration project. An activity such as this allows students to make a difference in their community and contribute to the field of science. As a result, students develop a positive attitude toward science and become confident in their ability to do science.

Karen Mesmer is a science teacher at Baraboo Middle School in Baraboo, Wisconsin.

Bitten by the Science Bug

By Viki Hymer

Who would have thought a primary level science camp would spark exciting science programs for the more than 1,000 elementary students in our school district in Stephenville, Texas. Not me, but it did.

After attending an astronomy camp at Tarleton State University (TSU) for teachers and secondary students in Summer 2002, I, a kindergarten teacher, was disappointed to discover that the university offered no science camps for elementary students.

I returned to my preK–K campus, whining to my principal. What a shame no one would take elementary—especially lower elementary—students seriously. Her reply was, "Then you do it. We'll do it." And we did, making a commitment then and there to strengthening students' science-process skills and teaching science inquiry at our school.

Starting Small, Thinking Big

We started small—we decided to host a summer science camp for 30 K–2 students in June 2003. I chose K–2 because I wanted to include more than one grade level. I did not target preK because I felt these students needed a bit more maturity before being in a class of 30 students.

For about three intense months, I did most of the planning with assistance from a preK teacher. We chose grade-appropriate activities for our camps, culling ideas from various Janice VanCleave books and Carson-Dellosa's Hands-On series of science books, the internet, and of course my own "bag of tricks" (see Resources). I also took advantage of the many professional development opportunities provided by the Fort Worth Museum of History and Science.

Camp registration forms were sent to every child in kindergarten, first, and second grade in the district. The camp was planned as a two-and-a-half hour camp each morning for five days. About 230 students signed up for a camp of 30 chairs!

Because of the obvious demand, the central office offered to fund teacher salaries for more camps if we were interested in conducting additional camps. We were. We added two more camps—another five-day morning camp and a shorter, three-day morning camp.

Next, we had to make the decisions as to who would attend the camps—that was the hardest part. We tried to include a cross-section of students: those interested in science; special education students; those who might not have as many opportunities as others; those whom we knew were very bright but labeled as at risk; students with low reading scores; English-as-a-second-language students who did not attend summer school; and classroom teacher suggestions. Letters of confirmation or "You are on a waiting list" were then sent to students. In all, 96 children attended the camps. Families were asked to pay a fee of $10 if possible. As we received more district support for the camp in following years, we were able not to charge any money for the camps.

Taking Over the Teachers' Lounge

Of course, the overwhelming response meant we needed a big enough place to have the camp. The principal offered the teachers' lounge and meeting room—a very large room with a kitchen area and closet at one end. The room was perfect, allowing students an area to work in and teachers an area for cleanup and storage. Materials were next on the agenda, and there we ran into the major problem of the whole project—money.

The principal had OK'd some funds from the school budget for the project, but, after studying catalogs, I realized that $6,000 would not go far. I tried to secure grants, but my requests for out-of-town grants went nowhere. Discouragement was setting in.

I wanted to get input from parents about my idea, so I asked parents from my classroom. They were very excited and the word spread. Eventually, parents and businesses in our community came forth with about $4,000 of support, and the project took off. In addition, we recruited some high school science students to volunteer to assist at the camps for community service credit, and one teacher volunteered to assist a few mornings the first week.

Summer of Science

Basically, the first camp was spent doing things I have always wanted to do in my classroom but never had time for. I had a blast. Even snack

time included science—we incorporated cooking activities that illustrated change, such as cooking donuts.

I settled on physics, astronomy, and chemistry as the theme for the first camp, naming it "PAC." I felt that these areas were the ones most elementary teachers seldom touched on. Chemistry and physics were covered for four days, and one day was devoted to astronomy with a visit to TSU's planetarium.

To open each day, we conducted a problem-solving activity with the whole group. The large-group problem-solving activities included how to get a nail out of a bottle of water without pouring out the water and how to discover what was in a ball of modeling clay without tearing it open. We also played games to define *force, constellations,* and the three forms of matter.

Afterward, we divided the children into two groups, one going into my classroom across from the lab for a structured experiment and one remaining in the lab for work with physics-type materials, building manipulatives, or computer science programs.

In chemistry, we conducted activities using soda, calcium carbonate, vinegar, and cabbage juice to illustrate chemical changes. In addition, we made silly putty and "oobleck," combined cornstarch and water, and did egg experiments that caused changes in their shells.

On astronomy day, in addition to the planetarium visit, we designed our own constellations and wrote stories about them.

Our physics explorations included magnet and force-and-motion activities, simple machines and bridge-building exercises, and creating bubbles to cover our whole bodies.

On one of the physics days, the children had to solve a problem. I rigged a water hose to be 80 cm away from a flower. Working in teams of four to five, the students had to build a device using mostly "trash" items that would allow the water to reach the flower. The students had to state their problem and describe and show how they solved it to two visitors from TSU, an engineering professor and planetarium director, who then awarded the students with an "Engineering Certificate." They were excited and took that excitement home. Parents were telling us they had trouble keeping their children out of the trash. They wanted to keep building.

At the end of every day, we sent home an experiment or activity the students could do at home with their parents. We also had a book fair the last day, making science books and materials available for the students to purchase.

The camps were a complete success. Calls from public school parents, home-schooling parents, and private school parents kept coming in during the camps asking if there were any no-shows. Kids were desperate to attend—science had definitely touched a nerve.

Expanding Horizons

Camp expansion was almost automatic. My original vision was to provide lower elementary students the same opportunities offered to secondary students. Though I started with my grade level, I had in mind that the camps would eventually expand up through the grade levels—and had presented this idea at the central office. With the success of our camps and the obvious excitement surrounding them, the central office was quickly supportive of the expansion efforts.

The camps that followed the first year had many changes. The biggest change was the creation of a dedicated science lab on the preK–K campus (see "Here Comes a Lab"). The 2003–2004 school year opened with plans to create new science opportunities for all elementary grades (up to fourth grade), and we planned six camps for grades K–4. The fifth- and sixth-grade campus also conducted its own camp last summer. Weekend science camps were also planned for third- and fourth-grade students, and an after-school enrichment (ASE) program was developed for first- through fourth-graders

to enhance their science skills. We unfortunately did not have room for all to attend. We keep a list of the students who sign up and who has attended which camp to allow each child to attend at least one camp.

To help with the expansion, I recruited a fourth-grade teacher to help teach the camps. Her expertise in math and science strengthened the content of the programs. The planning of the camps is becoming more organized. We cover a variety of state standards and subjects. Each month we target one standard, integrating other standards as appropriate. Lab plans with state standards for K–4 levels listed are written for the central office to share with teachers at the other schools. At our school, we are developing a lab manual with several labs for each state standard.

Lasting Results

Our efforts have paid off. Teachers are seeing an improvement of skills in the classroom. Students not previously interested in reading and writing are coming forth with independent studies, documenting observations in journals.

We also often seek input from students concerning their interests. We try to balance the camps with all areas of science—the first year was physics, astronomy, and chemistry. We followed that with biology—the kids clamored for dissections, so we did, cutting up more than 100 fish and earthworms. We also did comparison studies of crayfish, fish, and sea stars, and included two days on birds.

The weekend camps and ASE have included spiders around Halloween, simple machines, building a car for racing, plant studies, and a "whodunit" based on the elementary rap of "Who Took the Cookie From the Cookie Jar?" The sheriff is a good friend and his son is in our camps so, of course, we enlisted his help to arrest "the culprit." This summer we are studying rocks and fossils. Next school year (2005–2006), we are thinking about caves or bats around Halloween, eggs for spring, and

Here Comes a Lab

Our district's main administration office took notice of our successful camp efforts, realizing that we were indeed serious about doing science at the lower elementary level. In support, the district approved money to create a preK–K science lab on our campus.

The makeshift lab in the teachers' lounge soon gave way to a state-of-the-art laboratory, complete with furniture, shelves, computers, and materials that would be any science teacher's dream. The lab encompassed the whole teachers' lounge, kitchen, and storage room and included many new supplies. A colleague, a high school chemistry teacher, joked I had more materials in my lab than she had in hers.

I spent about one year planning and ordering for the lab. I planned the development of the lab in stages, with the intention it be completed in three years. We beat the deadline. By the end of June 2003, the indoor lab was complete and we were beginning to think of ways to expand to include outdoor learning.

To use the lab, each teacher is assigned an hour each week and may go more if the lab is not in use—although this is seldom. The teachers are responsible for their planning, and I developed a lab manual from which they can get ideas.

I am responsible for ordering materials, maintaining the organization of the lab, and making future plans for the lab—all with input from the other teachers. I also am available to assist teachers in planning if needed. An aide was hired to work in the lab daily, making it easier for kindergarten teachers by doing the lab setup and cleanup for their lab each week. The lab is also used for teacher training and workshops and for parent night for our school science fair.

Other grade levels have followed suit and are creating new science labs in their schools as well. Science is on our minds in our district.

weather for the summer camps. The possibilities are limitless.

The success of the preK–K lab has spurred me to "think outside the lab," and this year, with the help of the Tarleton University Horticulture Club, we are landscaping a large area outside the lab. A 4 m × 11 m sandpit has been put in for potential paleontological, archaeological, and Earth science studies. Small forest, desert, and grassland habitats are being developed as well as a wildflower and garden area. An area to house small animals for study is also in the works.

The science bug has spread throughout the district and beyond—today we are developing plans to encourage teachers to integrate science into reading and math. We are also planning to include Tarleton State University science and education students as volunteers. If kindergarten can affect science throughout our district, we can affect science all the way up to the university level. Touching future teachers will touch the future of science.

Viki Hymer is a kindergarten teacher in Stephenville, Texas.

Acknowledgment
Fellow teacher Donna Curtis and principal Judy Walker—also from Stephenville, Texas—were essential to the success of the science initiatives described in this article, with assistance from teachers Becky Hodges, Anita Chaplin, Kim Kaiser, and Sue Gray. Without their participation and support, the programs would not have occurred. Camper Jacob Woolridge, an aspiring biologist who is fighting neuroblastoma, inspired this article.

Resources
National Research Council (NRC). 1996. *National Science Education Standards*. Washington, DC: National Academy Press.

Parratore, P. 2001. *Hands-on chemistry*. Greensboro, NC: Carson-Dellosa.

VanCleave, J. 1991. *Physics for every kid*. New York: John Wiley and Sons.

VanCleave, J. 1993. *200 gooey, slippery, slimy, weird, and fun experiments.* New York: John Wiley and Sons.

Internet

Thinking Fountain: Science Museum of Minnesota
  www.sci.mus.mn.us/sln/tf
The Hands-On Technology Program
  www.galaxy.net/~k12/index.shtml
Exploratorium
  www.exploratorium.edu

Connecting to the Standards

This article relates to the following National Science Education Standards (NRC 1996):

Teaching Standards

Standard D: Teachers of science design and manage learning environments that provide students with the time, space, and resources needed for learning science.

Standard E: Teachers of science develop communities of science learners that reflect the intellectual rigor of scientific inquiry and the attitudes and social values conducive to science learning.

Program Standards

Standard D: The K–12 science program must give students access to appropriate and sufficient resources, including quality teachers, time, materials and equipment, adequate and safe space, and the community.

Girls in Science Rule!

By Jan E. Moore

The "great outdoors" was the learning ground at an exciting, activity-filled science camp for girls sponsored by educators from Eastern Kentucky University in Richmond. The overnight weekend camp, known as Girls in Science Rule!, was created for girls entering sixth grade who want to learn science and explore science-related fields.

The camp was developed specifically for this age group because is it often during the middle school years that children begin seriously considering career choices. And, even today, in the 21st century—though more females are majoring in the sciences and in engineering than ever before—women remain a minority in many scientific disciplines.

Camps like Girls in Science Rule!—with its activities that promote positive attitudes toward science, develop participants' science-process skills, and celebrate girls' and women's achievements in science—may lead more women to pursue careers in science, hopefully reducing the gender disparity in the field.

Life at Maywoods

Girls in Science Rule! was held at Maywoods, an environmental laboratory owned and operated by Eastern Kentucky University. Maywoods contains about seven square kilometers of wooded area, with a lake, lodge, and several hiking trails throughout the forest. The camp featured a range of environmental education experiences for participants, including indoor activities, such as using a microscope and a video flex camera, and outdoor activities, such as hiking and learning nature survival tips.

Students from Eastern Kentucky University—who were majoring in elementary education with a science emphasis—served as the camp's activity leaders or "trainers," receiving a small stipend for their efforts. The trainers led the girls through the activities and were the heart of the program. The trainers were excellent role models: They were young (so the girls related to them), female, and interested in science. And, they worked side by side with camp participants, modeling that women can do science successfully.

The lodge at Maywoods provided accommodations for the girls and trainers. The facility was equipped with a restaurant-style kitchen where all meals were prepared. Funding for the camp was obtained from Eastern Kentucky University and the Mid-South Educational Research Association, a nonprofit incorporated organization representing several southern states that encourages quality educational research in schools and institutions of higher learning.

As director of the camp, I was present at all times. I was the "woman behind the scenes." Primarily, I selected the trainers and activities, arranged transportation and lodging, provided support to trainers, and cooked and prepared meals and snacks. My role was to ensure that the event ran as smoothly as possible and that everyone had a positive learning experience.

'Scopes and Sights

When camp started, the girls were eager to explore Maywoods's forest and hiking trails. After a nature walk in the woods, the girls returned indoors to view under a microscope some of the items they had collected outdoors, such as insects and leaves with fungi.

The insects provided a wonderful source of amazement and amusement. Students used microscopes to view details of insect parts and dissecting scopes to examine entire insects, sticks, leaves, and trash. The girls were surprised at what they could learn about wildlife simply by studying evidence found on leaves. One student said, "I didn't know a leaf could be a home and food at the same time."

Next, we introduced what would be the girls' favorite gadget throughout the event, the video flex camera. We connected the camera to the television so all girls could view all of the objects. They viewed parts of a tarantula, a poison ivy lesion, and one participant's mouth, among numerous other interesting objects. They took advantage of every opportunity between activities to view other objects around the lodge.

Trail Know-How

Later in the camp, trainers taught the girls how to recognize and leave handmade signs on trails in the event that they got lost. For example, when faced with a fork in a trail, hikers should leave a sign indicating the path taken. One such sign might be to pile several sticks in the shape of an "X" in front of the chosen trail. Another might be to create a pile of rocks in the center of a trail, placing one or two rocks from the pile on the left side of the fork if they've chosen to take the left fork, or one or two rocks in the right side of the fork if they've chosen that direction.

Students were instructed to make the signs obvious, leaving little doubt that these could have occurred incidentally. The trainers discouraged the girls from creating trails of food or broken sticks, explaining that animals might eat the food, leaving no trail, and broken sticks are too common in the forest.

The trainers also shared tips about how to stay safe in the woods. For example, they provided the girls with information about how to identify poison ivy and poison oak and discussed the insects and snakes that could possibly be encountered in the area. They also instructed the girls never to leave the trails and to stay with their trainer.

Tracking Adventure

After learning the woods safety rules and practicing their trail signs, the girls participated in a tracking adventure to put their newfound skills to the test. The girls were divided into two groups of ten. Group One ventured out for a walk in the woods, selecting a route from the many available trails and leaving signs for Group Two to find and follow.

Group Two began tracking after giving the first group a 20-minute head start. As they came to forks in the trails, they had to decide which trail the first group had chosen. At first, the girls were unable to distinguish signs from incidental breakage in limbs and displacement of leaves. One girl exclaimed, "Hey look at this branch. It's broken!" Another stated, "Yeah, but that's not a real sign. Anything could have done that." Then, after being reminded to look for the specific signs they had been trained to use and recognize, they began distinguishing real signs from insignificant observations. Real signs left little or no doubt that they were left by the first group.

The girls were ecstatic when they were able to successfully track the others by applying what they had learned. You could hear them exclaiming, "Oh, look, this has got to be a sign!" while others were observing trails for evidence of foot tracks. As Group One heard Group Two coming up the trail, giggles were heard throughout the forest. When asked which activity participants enjoyed the most on an evaluation, this was their favorite activity. One girl commented, "I feel safer in the woods now." Another said, "I can teach my little sister this stuff!"

Pollution Solutions

Back at the lodge, students worked with a model that demonstrated how motor oil, insecticides, fertilizers, factory waste, and other substances can pollute a water supply. The plastic model looked like a small town, with topographical features such as houses, schools, farms, rivers, streams, and hills. It contained fluids that represented motor oil, pesticides, and fertilizers and provided narratives for teachers to follow, such as a farmer has spilled oil from his tractor and fertilizer is put on yards and golf courses. (Models like this can be purchased from a science supplier for about $1,000. Our school district owns one for teachers to check out for use in their classrooms.)

As the girls observed the model, the trainers asked such questions as

- "What do you think will happen to these pollutants when it rains?"
- "Where do you think these pollutants will go?"
- "How does this affect our ground water?"
- "What is a watershed?"

The girls then used a spray bottle filled with water to simulate rainfall and recorded their observations. The model demonstrated how rain washes away oil and fertilizers and then flows to other areas. The girls were surprised to discover how something put on a lawn, such as fertilizer, could affect the streams and rivers in the area.

Last, the group brainstormed ideas to reduce the amount of pollution produced by runoff. Some suggestions included properly discarding used oil, having a professional change the oil and properly discard the used oil, reducing the amount of fertilizers used on lawns, and doing away with fertilizers altogether.

Nighttime Thoughts

At night, girls sat outside on the lodge deck and created poems about their day, capturing their thoughts and feelings about their experience. This activity was another favorite among the girls. Afterward, those who wished to share their poems read them aloud. Figure 1 shows two students' examples.

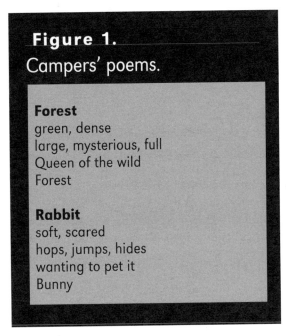

Figure 1.
Campers' poems.

Forest
green, dense
large, mysterious, full
Queen of the wild
Forest

Rabbit
soft, scared
hops, jumps, hides
wanting to pet it
Bunny

Poetry writing was a perfect end to the day. It was a quiet restful activity that helped settle the girls for sleep.

Attitudes and Success

Girls in Science Rule! provided a positive science learning experience for participants. Before camp began, we collected "attitude surveys" from each attendee. The surveys focused on participants' confidence and anxiety levels related to doing science. After the camp experience, they completed the survey again. The surveys revealed significantly more positive attitudes toward science after attending the camp than before it. When asked if they would be interested in attending similar program another time, all of the girls enthusiastically answered, "Yes!"

So, if you love science and you are interested in promoting science to girls, try planning a camp of your own—the earlier the better. We've recently begun developing programs targeting girls in elementary schools. Based on my own experience, I'm hopeful that these new programs and others like them will draw more and more women into the exciting world of science.

Jan E. Moore is an assistant professor of science education in the Department of Curriculum and Instruction at Eastern Kentucky University in Richmond, Kentucky.

Resources

Downing, J. E. 2002. The scientist within: You go girl! Paper presented at the Mid-South Educational Research Association, Little Rock, AR

Hixson, B. K. 1999. *Women in science rule!* Sandy, Utah: Loose in the Lab.

Lane, N. 1999. Why are there so few women in science? Nature Debates (available online at *www.nature.com/nature/debates/women/women_contents.html*) England: Macmillan.

National Research Council (NRC). 1996. *National Science Education Standards.* Washington, DC: National Academy Press.

Connecting to the Standards
This article relates to the following National Science Education Standards (NRC 1996):

Grades 5–8
Content Standards
Standard G: History and Nature of Science
• Science as human endeavor
• Nature of science

Section 4

The Family: Take-Home Projects and Family Science Events

The Family

Take-Home Projects and Family Science Events

Lynn Dierking has devoted her career to understanding and facilitating opportunities for out-of-school science, technology, engineering, and mathematics (STEM) learning. She states that

> At the core of this view is an important and meaningful role for parents, guardians and other significant adults in children's lives. Unfortunately, much lip service is paid to the importance of parent involvement and yet the barriers to parents truly engaging in their children's learning, particularly in school, are pervasive though subtle, as demonstrated by frameworks such as the ecologies of parental engagement (Barton et al. 2004; Dierking et al. 2005; McCreedy and Luke 2006). This is unfortunate because if significant adults better understood how important positive interactions with their infants and young children were, and how to facilitate those interactions, more children would grow up in intellectually stimulating environments.
>
> At the present, large segments of the U.S. population grow up deprived, not because of a lack of interest or desire on the part of parents and significant adults but due to a lack of parental experience and knowledge about how to optimize the learning potential of the home and connect it to their children's school experience. My research and that of others suggests that certainly not all, but many of these adults, can be empowered to better understand their roles and abilities as their children's first and most important educators, rather than feeling that the entire educational role is the responsibility of the schools or cultural institutions. Interestingly, these efforts also demonstrate that these adults enjoy participating in STEM activities and learning about STEM topics themselves. Ideally every significant adult in a child's life would be provided the support necessary to feel like competent educators rather than made to feel inadequate, as is often the case. In addition, every child would not only be a learner but also a teacher to their parents, rather than erroneously being told and shown daily that only adults have any knowledge worth communicating. (1997)

Research clearly indicates that parental involvement is a critical indicator of children's success in school. But many parents do not have access to the knowledge or ability to support the learning that begins at school. The NSTA position statement Parent Involvement in Science Education provides suggestions concerning how parents can be involved in their children's learning (NSTA 1994).

Parents should do the following:

- Let the child take the lead, and then build on his or her interests.
- Take time to "do" science, helping the child explore his or her world;
- talk with the child and listen to his or her explanations and questions instead of just giving answers;
- Be prepared to say "I don't know." Ask questions to help the child learn to search for solutions.
- Be enthusiastic! Let the child see your curiosity.
- Be ready for teachable moments.
- Teach safe habits as a way of life.
- Encourage the child's day-care facility or school to have science-related activities.
- Look for community organizations with science-related programs nearby and take advantage of these services.
- Explore science in the community. Visit such places as museums, airports, gardens, plants, dairies, farms, exhibitions, gravel pits, observatories, parks, planetariums, recycling centers, treatment plants, shorelines, and weather stations, and use their resources.
- Develop a resource library at home! Gather materials from bookstores, science museums, electronic bulletin boards. Collect computer programs, reference books, posters, databases, and so on.

If you are seeking a copy-and-paste, plug-and-go approach to designing family events for your school, this section is probably not for you. Rather it is a food-for-thought section providing a variety of ideas to engage you in thinking about how it can apply to your situation and needs.

In This Section *(articles are in italics)*

With the goal of exciting an entire community about science, *So, You Want To Host a Family Sci-ence Night?* uses science as a galvanizing force for the school community. This template provides explanations on how to develop activities that are entertaining as well as meaningful science experiences based on discrepant events. Planning by a team of event organizers is the main focus with all of the decisions to be made clearly outlined. Activities used by this team as well as additional activity sources are provided.

Parents, elementary students, university students and faculty, and elementary teachers come together for an evening of fun, science experiments, demonstrations, and activities. *A Science Night of Fun!* is a model that uses the help of university faculty and students in designing a science night that provides an opportunity to make science accessible and enjoyable for everyone. This step-by-step account of how the night was developed includes project planning, publicizing the event, setting up the event, activities conducted during the event, and outcomes. Take-home activities are provided to extend the learning after the event.

The final six short articles in this section concentrate on engaging parents and their children in science experiences at home or during family outings. They are ideal for referencing on a teacher web page or classroom newsletter.

Using materials and equipment easily found in all homes is one of the challenges facing teachers as they plan for at-home science experiences. Water is one of the most readily available resources for student investigations. At-home questions to investigate are provided in *Drop by Drop, Liter by Liter*, as students study water use and waste.

Firsthand investigation through the use of another easily obtained material is conducted in *Breaking the Code: Examining Your Mail*. Much as a detective solves a crime through clues, mail provides clues to its origins. This activity provides valuable connections to geography, classification, patterns, data collection, and inference versus observation.

Crime stopping and CSI are currently interesting topics for children. *Get Familiar With Fingerprints* is yet another investigation that uses easily found materials because students can use their own fingerprints or those of other family members. This article is one of many featured in the Home Zone column of *Science and Children*, see more in the journal's section of *www. NSTA.org.*

Selecting TV programming that supports learning is a challenge for families. Teachers can use this valuable tool and help families in these decisions with a little guidance. *Family Viewing* provides a glimpse into how one family uses TV and internet sites for science learning.

Many parents want to know how to focus their child's attention when visiting informal science locations. *Museums as Inquiry Role Models* provides ideas teachers can use to support positive learning experiences by families.

One response to the question of engaging students in science while on vacation is provided in *Capitalizing on Student Travel in Earth Science Classrooms.* The ideas in this article are adaptable to other content areas and support learning on extended time away from school.

References

Barton, A. C., C. Drake, J. G. Perez, K. St. Louis, and M. George. 2004. Ecologies of parental engagement in urban education. *Educational Researcher* 33: 3–12.

Dierking, L. 1997. Linking after-school programs and STEM learning: A view from another window. Guest editorial. *Science Education.* 8 (6).

Dierking, L. D., M. Storksdieck, S. Foutz, K. Haley Goldman, M. Wadman, and C. Kessler. 2005. Families exploring science together (FEST). Summative evaluation report. Annapolis, MD: Unpublished technical report.

McCreedy, D. and J. J. Luke. 2006. *Using science to bridge the learning gap between home and school.* In *Teaching and learning science: A handbook.* Vol. 2, 393–400), K. Tobin, ed. Connecticut: Praeger.

National Science Teachers Association (NSTA). 1994. NSTA position statement: Parent involvement in science education. *www.nsta.org/ about/positions.aspx*

Resources

The articles listed are available through the Learning Center on the NSTA web site at *http://learningcenter.nsta.org.*

Criminale, C., N. Esfan, and M. Mathew. 2006. Energy bowlerama. *Science Scope* 30: 30–33.

Farenga, S. J., and D. Ness. 2006. Calories, energy, and the food you eat. *Science Scope* 29: 50–52.

Hogan, T., and J. Craven. 2005. They're here! A coast-to-coast investigation of invasive species. *Science Scope* 29: 62–64.

Joyce, B., and S. Farenga. 1999. The neurological tourist. *Science Scope* 23: 40–41.

Wolfinger, D. 2005. Project produce. *Science and Children* 28: 26–29.

So, You Want to Host a Family Science Night?

By Cynthia Lundeen

This is the year you're going to get your class—maybe even the whole community—excited about science. At the very least, you're going to involve more parents in the science curriculum—but how? With the exception of periodic science fairs or the occasional home-science project, science is not usually a galvanizing force for the school community. But, through family science events, it can be.

It's no secret that students whose families are involved in their children's education significantly benefit in achievement, attitudes, and application. Academic and anecdotal research clearly indicates parent involvement is a critical predictor of children's school success (Lazar et al. 1999). But, often, as Tichenor (1998, p. 248) asserts, "the greatest barrier to parental involvement is the lack of knowledge of schools and families on how to effectively work and plan together." Well, don't let that barrier hold you back any longer. Using the following template as a guide, you can host a successful family science event at your school. Don't worry. Just do it!

All in the Family

The concept of *family science* is just as its name implies—a way to introduce science concepts to students and their parents through hands-on activities that allow families to learn and work together. I've found discrepant events—science experiences in which the outcomes are counterintuitive and often a surprise—to be especially effective when used as part of a family science effort. Discrepant events probe, challenge, and clarify observers' current ideas (Crockett 2004). After viewing the event—for example, an extinguished candle suddenly relights without a match or a seltzer tablet mixed with soda pops the top of a film canister—participants then learn the science explanation behind the event, promoting meaningful learning. See Figures 1 and 2 for examples of discrepant events appropriate for a family science night.

In addition to helping families share meaningful learning experiences together, family science events can be helpful in meeting other important needs for your school:

Figure 1.
Discrepant events.

Blast-off Bottle Rockets! (*adapted from stevespanglerscience.com*)
Blast-off Bottle Rockets! For Parents and Children
When Alka-Seltzer® tablets combine with carbonated soda, carbon dioxide is released. Demonstrating this phenomenon is simple: Add soda to a film canister with one Alka-Seltzer tablet, snap on the lid, and observe. The carbon dioxide gas builds up and the homemade bottle rocket blasts off!

ATTENTION SCIENTISTS: This event requires protective safety glasses. Adult participation is required.

Materials
35 mm film canisters with snap-on lids (Clear canisters allow viewing of the chemical change)

Alka-Seltzer tablets—one per canister	Carbonated soda
Saftey goggles or glasses	Timer or watch
Paper towels	Meterstick
Record-keeping sheet	Large bowl

Observation: What Happens When ... ?
Put on safety glasses.
Predict then observe what happens when an Alka-Seltzer tablet is dropped in water. Encourage verbal description of the physical change.
Predict and observe what happens when an Alka-Seltzer tablet is dropped in soda.
Participants verbalize the differences in the chemical change.

Concept Development: Chemical Change Produces CO_2
Participants learn that water and an Alka-Seltzer tablet produce carbon dioxide (CO_2) as a result of a chemical reaction. With the soda, the production of CO_2 is enhanced by the carbonation already IN the soda, producing a more reactive chemical change.

Concept Application: Let's Try It!
Participants find evidence of carbon dioxide produced by the chemical reaction through this hands-on experiment.
Predict what will happen if a lid or top is placed on the two solutions.
Fill one film canister half full with seltzer water.
Drop one Alka-Seltzer tablet into the canister and quickly seal it.
Place canister in a large bowl and move away to observe what happens.
Measure time it takes until "blast-off" and record.
Be sure to aim away from eyes and others.
BLAST-OFF!
After blast-off, locate lid and measure distance from the bowl. Record.
Recall what causes the explosion ... the release of carbon dioxide in a chemical change!

Extensions:
Do varying the amounts of liquid/Alka-Seltzer change the results?
Try it!
Record, graph, and compare results. Draw conclusions.

Figure 2.
More discrepant events.

Sorda Pop! (Adapted from _Glide into Winter with Math and Science_, Shirley et al. 1987)
Sorda Pop! For Parents and Children
When soda pop is mixed with vinegar or a liquid with high acidic content, carbon dioxide is formed. When confined to a container, the gas builds up, pressure forms and pushes outward. You can demonstrate this with a water bottle and balloon to the amazement of the audience!

ATTENTION SCIENTISTS: This event should be monitored by adults.

Materials
Empty water bottles (small ones work well!)
Balloons   Baking soda
Small funnel   White vinegar
Water   Styrofoam cups*
Fruit juice

*Prepare Ahead:
Fill deflated balloons with 2 teaspoons of baking soda using the funnel. Pour ¼ cup of vinegar into the empty water bottle. Carefully stretch the mouth of the balloon over the top of the water bottle, avoiding spilling any of the baking soda into it. Prepare as many as you will need for participants.

Observation: What Happens When ... ?
Provide a premade balloon bottle to participants. Predict what will happen when the balloon is turned upright and the baking soda falls into the "water." The balloon will inflate as the gas is released inside the bottle! What happened? Encourage verbal description of the physical change.

Concept Development
CO_2 is dispersed in a chemical change. Participants learn that the "water" is actually vinegar and the gas buildup causes pressure that is evident by the inflation of the balloon. Explain that the same gas (carbon dioxide) is found in everyday soft drinks that they drink.

Concept Application: Let's Try It!
Participants find evidence of carbon dioxide by making a soft drink out of juice. Predict what will happen when they attempt to make their own "sorda-pop." Pour ½ cup of juice into Styrofoam cups. Participants can measure ¼ teaspoon of baking soda and add to juice. The juice will "sorda" look like soda pop, complete with bubbles and fizz. Compare with "real" soda by pouring into another cup and comparing results of the carbon dioxide dispersion. Recall what causes the chemical reaction ... the release of carbon dioxide in a chemical change!

Extensions
What other places are gases formed? Any other food or drink products? Are there other liquids that would have the same results?
Try it!
Record, graph, and compare results. Draw conclusions.

- Bringing members of home, school, and community together to promote science education;
- Providing an accessible science learning environment for multicultural populations; and
- Demonstrating connections between science education, career choices, and gender equity.

Planners Unite!

With such positive outcomes at stake, you're probably eager to plan an event that meets your school's particular needs. To begin, assemble a group of interested individuals and form a planning committee. Typically, this team contains two to four representatives each from parent and community groups and local universities along with teachers, science coordinators, and school administrators.

Each member of the team will likely have particular areas of expertise in which he or she excels, so a good idea is to divide the volunteers into groups and assign organizational tasks appropriate to each person's skills:

- core planning
- participant recruitment
- professional development
- materials and context preparation
- peripherals and vendors

Although there may be some overlap in the tasks done among groups, typical responsibilities in each group are described below.

When, Where, Who, and How

The core planning group makes the broad decisions regarding the event, such as choosing the date, time, and location for the event; deciding who the event is for (i.e., specific grade levels or the entire school population or community); and determining whether the event will be a one-time event or several events held weekly, monthly, or at intermittent times during the year. Each variation has its benefits, and your school's specific needs will determine the best choice.

Having the event at the school creates an inviting atmosphere in which parents and children feel comfortable and welcome. Depending on participant numbers and the time of the year, family science night can be held outdoors if the school facility permits. Usually, gymnasiums and cafeterias are the venues of choice,

although smaller areas such as classrooms can be used as well.

Family Science events can be stand-alone features during the school year or occur in conjunction with other major school events, such as open houses, parent-teacher organization meetings, and community collaborative events, such as fall festivals or spring flings. For a first-time event, combining a family science night with an already established event may improve attendance.

Core planners are also responsible for securing funding for the event. This can mean accessing money earmarked from a school budget or coming up with ideas for extra activities, such as book fairs or refreshment stands. Providing food is an always popular fund-raiser. Parent-school organizations or local vendors may want to sell pizzas, hot dogs, and soft drinks as a fund-raiser. Alternatively, I have found a call to parents for snack donations always reaps more than enough for event snacks.

Finally, core planners decide on advertising and incentives to encourage attendance at the event, such as door prizes, raffles, T-shirts, or student attendance incentives, such as a "freedom-from-homework" pass or a best-class-attendance ice cream treat award. Short parent seminars for at-home science activities are excellent ideas for parent attendance incentive.

We Want You

People tasked with recruiting participants are responsible for locating volunteers—parents, teachers, university students or professors, scientists—to lead discrepant events workshops. Parents also recruit community members—such as museum docents, meteorologists, and hobbyists—who may want to share their science expertise in other ways, such as by providing a related science display or exhibit.

Seek volunteers by distributing flyers and making phone calls, or by sending guest speakers to other school and parent meetings. High

Figure 3.
Science activity resources.

Invitations to Science Inquiry 2nd Edition by Tik L. Liem. 1992. Chino Hills, CA: Science Inquiry Enterprises.

This fascinating book for science teachers contains more than 400 discrepant events to motivate students in learning science. It is specifically designed and written for elementary, junior high, and senior high school teachers.

Showy Science: Exciting Hands-on Activities That Explore the World Around Us; Grades Three to Six by Hy Kim. 2000. Parisppany, NJ: Celebration Press.

More than 175 exciting, hands-on science demonstrations that WORK using ordinary household objects. Students explore water, air, animals, plants, microbes, gravity and motion, Earth, and light as they show off scientific principles for their classmates and friends.

202 Science Investigations: Exciting Adventures in Earth, Life, and Physical Sciences by Marjorie Frank. 1990. Nashville, TN: Incentive Publications.

Welcome students to the amazing world of science with the easy-to-use activities in this resource. No elementary classroom is complete without this collection. Most of the activities require no science apparatus, just easily collectable everyday materials.

Steve Spangler Science, *www.stevespangler science.com*

These eye-catching demonstrations and activities help teachers pursue the "why-factor" of wonder, discovery, and exploration.

school students are particularly willing to present fun science activities and can be offered service hours needed for graduation requirements. Local science professionals such as weather reporters can be excellent presenters as well as crowd pleasers. Keep diversity in mind when recruiting—presentations in other languages can be highly successful due to the hands-on nature of each science event. This also accomplishes the goal of encouraging science careers for all members of a school community.

"Training" Workshop

Once you've assembled the participants, the coordinators should schedule a training workshop in which the event planning committee and any recruited experts—high school science teachers, university instructors, and elementary teachers, for example—model discrepant events for the volunteers and show them how to lead the hands-on activities.

After selecting a workshop time convenient for most volunteers (often the biggest challenge in planning the event), assemble numerous sources for activities, including school science curricula, science activity books, and websites (see Figure 3 for a list of resources in which you can find activities appropriate for family science night).

Discrepant events are usually preselected by event planners from various science books and resources and presenters can then select from this array of events. I encourage presenters to choose an event they are interested in and feel comfortable presenting. The total number of events depends on your participants, resources, and pool of presenters. To keep the focus on doing science, I find a one-to-two-hour time limit is effective regardless of the number of events offered.

We use a variation of Koballa's Teaching Model for Discrepant Events in our workshop to coincide with a three-phase learning cycle model (Chiapetta and Koballa 2002):

1. Setting Up the Discrepant Event (*exploration*):
   Confront participants with questions or problems that gain attention, increase motivation, pose questions, and reveal misconceptions.
2. Resolving the Questions Posed by the Event and Relate Them to Science Knowledge (*concept development*):
   Participants will resolve the event themselves or learn with teacher assistance.
3. Active Involvement in Solving the Discrepancy (*application*):
   Participants engage in purposeful activity in attempting to resolve the discrepancy and/or apply to like situations to ensure understanding and links to their world.

The remainder of workshop time is spent answering questions concerning events. Each presenter receives a copy of a description of their event to take with them and a detailed outline of family science night.

Prep the Materials

Once the volunteers have chosen the discrepant events to conduct, getting the materials is the next step. Funds typically are provided from school science consumable budgets and parent donations or from parent-teacher organizations or other partnership funds. Depending on the size of the family science event, the rule of thumb is to budget for $10 per event. Some events may require more consumable materials, while other events have no cost, therefore setting this average.

Inform presenters to expect to repeat their event 10 to 20 times in one hour depending on the event. Gauge amounts of materials needed by calculating units of consumable materials needed for one demonstration times 20.

When the materials are purchased, the planning team and participants gather and distribute materials for events and prepare the location—this includes both the event space and parking.

I ask presenters to provide a list of each event on an index card with their name and their specific event name. Event planners then purchase needed materials and organize them in brown grocery bags with the index card stapled at the top. These "discrepant event bags" are then distributed to participants either by self pickup or delivery.

Don't forget to allow enough time for practice among your presenters before family science night to iron out any problems or concerns before the big night!

And the Rest

Once the science events are in the hands of the presenters, the event planners' job is to ensure all participants arrive, set up, and do their thing. I ask all participants to be on-site and set up 30 minutes before students and their families arrive. Tables, lights, water sources, vendor areas, decorations, and refreshment areas can be established with the aid of school personnel prior to the arrival of the event presenters.

Some useful tips for event planners to keep things running smoothly include greeting parents and children at the entrance, asking parents to sign in, and distributing an event checklist for families as they enter the venue. A welcome announcement by school officials or planners signals the start of family science night. Door-prize tickets can be distributed or purchased and can be awarded throughout the evening. A concluding thank you and good night announcement ends family science night on a uniform note. My general rule is that no participants leave until cleanup is completed—a highly successful strategy to ensure a speedy departure by all.

A Night to Remember

Parent surveys I've collected after various family science nights have been overwhelmingly positive and indicate a strong desire for more such science school-home events. In this age of scientific knowledge explosion, effective science teaching and learning is dependent on such collaborations to help turn out our best scientists yet! With appropriate planning, your family science event can truly be a "Night to Remember."

Cynthia Lundeen is an assistant professor of education at Florida State University in Tallahassee, Florida.

Resources

Chiappetta, E. L., and T. R. Koballa. 2002. *Science instruction in the middle and secondary schools.* Upper Saddle River, NJ: Merrill/Prentice Hall.

Crockett, C. 2004. What do kids know—and misunderstand—about science? *Educational Leadership* 61 (5): 34–37.

Lazar, A., P. Broderick, T. Mastrilli, and F. Slostad. 1999. Educating teachers for parent involvement. *Contemporary Education* 70 (3): 5–10.

National Research Council (NRC). 1996. *National Science Education Standards.* Washington, DC: National Academy Press.

Shirley F., J. Nikoghosian, C. Peterson, J. Ewing, R. Adair, D. Smith, S. Mercier, and S. Wiebe. 1987. *Glide into winter with math and science.* Fresno, CA: AIMS Education Foundation.

Tichenor, M. S. 1998. Preservice teachers' attitudes towards parent involvement: Implications for teacher education. *The Teacher Educator* 33 (4): 248–259.

Connecting to the Standards

This article relates to the following National Science Education Standards (NRC 1996):

Teaching Standards

Standard A:
Teachers of science plan an inquiry-based science program for their students.

Standard B:
Teachers of science guide and facilitate learning.

A Science Night of Fun!

By Katie Rommel-Esham and Andrea Castellitto

Every spring, K–5 students from a local elementary school look forward to participating in Science Night. Science Night is an opportunity for members of our educational community to come together and enjoy science learning from a new perspective—one that takes science outside the classroom walls. Sponsored by State University of New York College (SUNY) at Geneseo in Geneseo, New York, this project brings together elementary students, parents, and university students and faculty for an evening of fun, meaningful science experiments, demonstrations, and activities.

Because science learning is often confined to a classroom, Science Night presents science experiences in a new setting with the purpose of making science accessible and enjoyable to everyone. Our university's Science Night program could easily serve as a model for any school interested in generating enthusiasm for science among teachers, students, and parents.

Science Night has its roots in the Family Math program that our university's school of education implements each fall in conjunction with a local elementary school. Since response to Family Math night was so great, we decided to host a similar evening with a focus on science. We hoped Science Night would give students and their parents an opportunity to interact with science topics in a new way. Our goal was to show participants that they can interact, learn something new, and incorporate science into everyday situations.

Project Planning

As with any large project, the first step involved detailed planning. About two months before the event, I selected an undergraduate student to coordinate the event and start planning—choosing activities, creating materials lists, and getting documents ready to be photocopied. From my perspective as event organizer, having a preservice teacher as coordinator was a lifesaver. She helped perform many of the tasks, like photocopying and e-mailing the other teacher candidates who were involved. She also determined which activities were appropriate for the event and which should go home with the students (this was mostly a question of physical logistics—we couldn't plant a garden in the cafeteria, for example). (See "Take-Home Activities.")

Next, interested parties—the undergraduate coordinator, a college faculty member, a parent council representative from the participating school, and a fourth-grade teacher—met over a two-week period and selected the activities. We planned on having about six weeks from initial planning to the night of the event, so things wouldn't be rushed. We chose 11 activities from various sources (see Resources).

The planning group tried to include a variety of lessons and topics so that everyone involved connected on some level to at least one activity. The group used the national and state learning standards, district curriculum, and the interests of students as a guide for choosing the activities. These guidelines helped the group relate the activities to students' science classroom content.

We began recruiting college volunteers approximately one month ahead of time. We found that it was unnecessary to offer students in methodology courses incentives such as extra credit to participate in such events—once the word was out, the students reminded us that they wanted to help.

Once the activities were chosen, the preservice teachers worked in pairs to prepare the lessons. They worked over a two-week period making posters advertising their activities, re-searching any background information related to their activities, and preparing to implement the activities—essentially doing a dry run to make sure everything worked as they thought it would. Methods instructors provided the preservice teachers with copies of their activity sheets and other resources so they could familiarize themselves with the activity and its related scientific principles. The school of education, the elementary parent council, and the school district provided additional support.

Getting the Word Out

The parent council, a cosponsor of the event, was responsible for advertising, collecting intent-to-attend sheets, providing refreshments, securing the room, and making the appropriate arrangements with the school district. They also helped with setting up before and cleaning up after the event and provided funding for any materials that were needed.

Elementary teachers were also involved in the advertisement at the classroom level—providing students with general information about the event, giving students assignments of things to look for as they participated or offering a homework bonus coupon for attendance.

Teachers wanted to actively recruit upper elementary (grades 3–5) students. Often, parents of younger, but not of older, students are willing to come to family learning events. Sparking these students' interest in attending worked well for the intermediate-aged group.

The Event

When Science Night arrived, the teacher candidates set up the room and distributed the necessary materials. The school cafeteria tables were arranged in a semicircular formation to allow students and their families to move easily around the room and to make sure there was plenty of space for a small group to participate

Take-Home Activities

How Do You Make an Egg Float?
An exploration of how adding salt to water affects density.

Two Water Towers
An exploration of how water tower size affects flow rate.

Trick Straw Race
An investigation of the effect of placing pinpoint holes in a drinking straw.

Science Night Activities

All Grades:
The Rainstick—Students make rainsticks using paper towel tubes and nails and experiment to see how different filler materials (unpopped popcorn kernels, rice, beans, split peas) produce different sounds.

Kazoo—Students use toilet paper tubes and waxed paper to create kazoos.

Secret Message—Students create messages with lemon juice and milk.

Kindergarten:
Bean Sprouts—Students examine lima beans from sprouting bean to growing plant.

Rubbings—What details can be enhanced by creating crayon rubbings of natural objects?

First grade:
Full Cup—How does surface tension affect the number of paper clips you can drop into a full glass of water?

Goo—Students investigate the properties of liquids and solids using cornstarch and water.

Popping Ping-Pong Balls—How many pennies do you need to make a Ping-Pong ball sink?

Second grade:
Hearing Things—Sound changes as it travels from spoons hitting a table through a string to our ears.

Spinning Colors—Can black and white really make colors?

Third grade:
Skin Prints—What kind of fingerprints do you have?

Tasting Center—Students examine where different kinds of taste buds are located.

Fourth grade:
Faking Fossils—Students "create" fossils with natural materials and plaster of paris.

An Oily Mess—Students investigate the effect of an "oil spill" on the environment.

Fifth grade:
Copter—Using paper and paper clips, students investigate aerodynamics and what factors affect the flight of their "helicopter."

Which Drops Faster?—Does an object's mass affect how quickly it will fall?

in each activity. Along with the activity tables, there was also a sign-in table and an estimation table.

At the back of the cafeteria, a refreshment table was set up with fruit, cookies, and juice for the participants to enjoy as the evening progressed. As a souvenir of the evening, "science wizard" stickers and bookmarks were also distributed.

As the students arrived and signed in, they received manila folders—prepared by the undergraduate event coordinator and another preservice teacher candidate—with directions for each of the evening's science activities as well as directions for a few activities to try on their own at home. Students could refer to these folders as they made their way through the activities.

Students signed in by using a dichotomous key to find their place in the chart. This helped—whether students knew it or not—to reinforce the ideas of categorization and well-defined sets. At the estimation table, primary-age students guessed the number of miniature candy bars and intermediate-level students guessed the number of chocolate kisses. These required minimal preparation and setup, yet served to reinforce an important concept for all of the students. In all cases, the estimates were written on sticky notes and used to create a bar graph. The winners—who took home the goody jars—were revealed toward the end of the evening.

Once inside, participants began their journey into various science activities and projects. Students and their families investigated the properties of "goo," made parachutes, made energy shift from potential to kinetic, tested the effect of gravity on falling objects, created rainsticks, explored their taste buds, examined sprouting lima beans at various stages, played with Cartesian divers, examined their fingerprints, and conducted many other activities (see "Science Night Activities"). The wide range of science experiences engaged both children and parents.

Parents responded positively to the activities and were involved on all levels. Our idea for this event was that parents not simply act as observers but actually participate along with their children. We wanted them to leave with the understanding that they can support their children in science learning at home with readily found materials.

To that end, the preservice teacher candidates who led the activities were instructed to facilitate the interactions between the elementary students and their parents and not be the ones who guided them through the activities—that was the role of their parents.

Parents responded well to this and seemed glad to have the opportunity to interact with their children in this way. All evening, mothers and fathers stood on chairs and dropped things, played with the goo, and made rainsticks alongside their children—they learned and had fun!

Positive Reinforcement

Participation in Science Night provided a variety of positive experiences for all involved. The teacher candidates were able to work with students in an informal setting that was comfortable and relaxed. Planning the event also enabled them to examine their own understanding of the science concepts presented throughout the night.

For many of the teacher candidates, the success of Science Night reinforced their decision to become teachers. Many teachers discovered that Science Night provided an intrinsic reward in much the same way that classroom teaching does.

The students also had a positive experience. They were excited by the enthusiasm the teacher candidates showed for the material they were presenting and did not hesitate to ask questions or challenge information they did not understand. Many were caught up in the idea of working with the older, "cooler" students. Still others seemed excited to be involved in a learning experience with their parents.

Parents Learn Too!

Throughout the event we emphasized the idea that parents can engage in meaningful science experiences with their children.

Because the parents jumped in and explored the science concepts along with their children, we hoped that this would help develop camaraderie and spark an interest in science that will be carried outside the walls of the school building. Indeed, many parents commented that they had forgotten how much fun science learning could be and how easily it could be done as a family.

Parents were glad to have an opportunity to interact with their children in a way that was different from simply helping with homework. They felt that Science Night enabled them to actually take part in their children's learning. Several parents commented that they didn't realize that so many things were considered science and said that they would start including children in home activities that support science learning, such as cooking and baking, gardening, and other things that require problem solving.

All in all, Science Night helped the elementary students, preservice teachers, parents, and classroom teachers gain a new perspective of science—they discovered learning science is an active process that is hands-on as well as minds-on and can be accomplished in ways other than traditional textbook learning.

The teacher candidates had the opportunity to try out some of the strategies they had learned in classes, which reinforced the usefulness of a process-oriented approach to teaching and learning. Many participants left Science Night with the realization that science is a vital, dynamic subject.

Katie Rommel-Esham is an assistant professor of mathematics and science education in the Ella Cline Shear School of Education at SUNY College at Geneseo in Geneseo, New York. Andrea Castellitto is a sixth-grade inclusion teacher in Somers Central School District in Somers, New York.

Resources

Bosak, S. V. 1998. *Science is ... a source book of fascinating facts, projects, and activities.* Ontario, Canada: Scholastic Canada.

Churchill, E. R., L. V. Loeschnig, and M. Mandell. 1998. *365 more simple science experiments with everyday materials.* New York: Workman.

Kenda, M., and P. S. Williams. 1992. *Science wizardry for kids.* New York: Scholastic.

National Research Council (NRC). 1996. *National Science Education Standards.* Washington, DC: National Academy Press.

Potter, J. 1995. *Science in seconds for kids.* New York: Scholastic.

Stenmark, J. K., V. Thompson, and R. Cossey. 1986. *Family math.* Berkeley, CA: Lawrence Hall of Science.

Tolman, M. N., and G. R. Hardy. 1999. *Discovering elementary science: Method, content, and problem-solving activities.* Needham Heights, MA: Allyn and Bacon.

Connecting to the Standards
This article addresses the following National Science Education Standards (NRC 1996):

Teaching Standards
Standard A: Teachers of science plan an inquiry-based science program for their students.

Standard B: Teachers of science guide and facilitate learning.

Standard D: Teachers of science design and manage learning environments that provide students with the time, space, and resources needed for learning science.

Standard F: Teachers of science actively participate in the ongoing planning and development of the school science program.

Professional Development Standards
Standard A: Professional development for teachers of science requires learning essential science content through perspectives and methods of inquiry.

Standard B: Professional development for teachers of science requires integrating knowledge of science, learning, pedagogy, and students; it also requires applying that knowledge to science teaching.

Standard C: Professional development for teachers of science requires building understanding and ability for lifelong learning.

Science Education Program Standards
Standard B: The program of study in science for all students should be developmentally appropriate, interesting, and relevant to students' lives; emphasize student understanding through inquiry; and be connected with other school subjects.

Standard C: The science program should be coordinated with the mathematics program to enhance student use and understanding of mathematics in the study of science and to improve student understanding of mathematics.

Standard D: The K–12 program must give students access to appropriate and sufficient resources, including quality teachers, time, materials, and equipment, adequate and safe space, and the community.

Standard E: All students in the K–12 science program must have equitable access to opportunities to achieve the National Science Education Standards.

Standard F: Schools must work as communities that encourage, support, and sustain teachers as they implement an effective science program.

Drop by Drop, Liter by Liter

By Stephen J. Farenga, Beverly A. Joyce, and Daniel Ness

It can be found as a solid, liquid, or gas. It is cohesive, colorless, tasteless, odorless, and has a pH of 7. These are some of the properties of pure water. Life without water would be unimaginable. Water is one of the most important substances for organisms on Earth. It is so important as a means of sustaining life that its existence is one of the first things that scientists look for on other planetary bodies.

The formula H_2O represents water's chemical structure of two positively charged hydrogen atoms covalently bonded to a negatively charged oxygen atom. Due to polarity, water molecules have a mutual attraction known as a hydrogen bond. A hydrogen bond occurs when the oppositely charged ends of the molecules are attracted to one another. In the case of water, the positively charged hydrogen ends of the molecule have an attraction for the negative oxygen atom of another molecule. This special bonding is responsible for many of water's unique qualities.

Water is essential in agriculture, manufacturing, and the home. Based on the characteristics of the local environment, the availability of this resource affects the distribution of populations. In fact, much of the debate regarding economic growth surrounds the availability of this resource. The water that we use in our homes comes from either a below-ground source (well or aquifer) or from a surface source (reservoir, river, or lake). According to the most recent United States Geological Survey Report in 1995, domestic consumption of water reached approximately 26.1 billion gallons per day. Even though these numbers are impressive, they have little practical meaning to us until we are confronted with periods of drought. It is evident from our reliance on water that conservation is imperative.

At-Home Questions to Investigate

How is water used in your home? Most people often do not realize the number of times they use an appliance that relies on water. In this investigation, students will be asked to monitor the frequency of home water use (see Figure 1). How many times are the sink, bathtub, shower, dishwasher, or washing machine used? To answer this question, students will need to monitor water appliance use for a selected period of time.

How much water is actually used? After calculating the frequency of water use, have students discuss how to calculate the volume of water consumed for each household task. It should become evident that certain appliances use a set volume of water to complete a house-

Structured Lesson Outline

Objective
You will be able to calculate the volume of water wasted from a leaking faucet.

Suggested materials
- Measuring cup or a graduated cylinder with milliliter (mL) units
- Liter container
- Pencil and paper
- Calculator
- Stopwatch or clock with second hand

Procedure
1. Discuss the importance of water and the need for conservation as a class.
2. Estimate how much water is wasted by a dripping faucet in a given time period. Determine a method for capturing, measuring, and calculating the actual amount of water wasted.
3. If no leaky faucet is available, turn on a faucet to create a slow drip, or the drip can be simulated using an eye dropper. With the leaky faucet/eye dropper, container with water, and a beaker, decide how to calculate the amount of water that is wasted by a leaking faucet.
4. Calculate and complete a sample wasted water collection chart (Figure 2). Time how long it takes to collect 25 mL, 50 mL, 100 mL, 250 mL, 500 mL, and 1,000 mL (1 liter). Extrapolate the length of time it would take to collect 10,000 mL (10 liters). Be sure to recycle the water you collect by watering plants when you are finished.
5. Calculate the amount of water wasted in one hour, 12 hours, 24 hours (one day), and one week (168 hours).
6. From the data collected, discuss the reasons why it is important to repair even small leaks and drips.

hold chore (washing machine or dishwasher, for example), while the amount of water used by other appliances depends on the duration of use (shower and shower head or sink and faucet, for example). Upon completing water-use surveys, engage students in a discussion to share ideas about how much water is being wasted in the home (Figure 2). Students may also use the established estimates from Figure 3 (based on data from the United States Geological Survey) to complete the activity. Some students may reply that water is wasted from defective faucets that drip. The situation of a leaking faucet can lead to an interesting scientific inquiry where students have the opportunity to discuss, hypothesize, measure, calculate, and extrapolate ways to practice water conservation (see "Structured Lesson Outline").

Have students determine a method for calculating the amount of water wasted by a dripping faucet. To do this, students need to answer two simple questions prior to conducting the investigation: "How does one gather and measure the dripping water?" and, "What is the amount of time needed to collect the water?"

There are a variety of options teachers can employ to complete the investigation. A more direct approach is to supply specific instructions to complete the tasks at hand. This works well for students who may not have adult guidance or a great deal of experience with finding and solving problems. The activity sheet on page 42 provides a framework to help students complete the investigation. The second option is to allow for open-ended inquiry. In general, this method requires the students to identify the problem, establish the procedures, and employ evaluative techniques needed for the investigation. In addition to these investigation possibilities, here are some ideas for potential extensions:

- Investigate how water gets into the home.
- Identify which agencies regulate the water quality in the community.

Figure 1.
Frequency of home water use over _____ time period.

Number of times used	Frequency of home water use over _____ time period.						
10							
9							
8							
7							
6							
5							
4							
3							
2							
1							
	Sink	Bathtub	Shower	Dishwasher	Washing machine	Toilet	Other

Figure 2.
Leaking water collection chart.

Name of water appliance:	Amount of H$_2$O lost		
Time (in minutes)	Milliliters	Liters	Kiloliters
1			
5			
10			
15			
20			
25			
30			

Figure 3.
Daily per person consumption of water estimates.

Type of water use	Amount of water (in liters)	Amount of water (in gallons)
Bath	189.270	50
Shower	7.571 (per minute)	2
Teeth brushing	3.785	1
Hands/face washing	3.785	1
Face/leg shaving	3.785	1
Dishwasher	75.708 (per load)	20
Dishwashing by hand	18.927 (per load)	5
Clothes washing	37.854 (per load)	10
Toilet flushing	11.356 (per flush)	3
Glasses of water drunk	Approx. 1/4 of 1 liter (250 ml)	8 ounces (0.0625 gal.)

* It should be noted that the amounts given in the table are only estimates of possible water consumption. Newer homes may have water saving appliances that help conserve the amount of water used. In addition, the amount of water used in conducting tasks like brushing teeth and washing hands can vary greatly if an individual leaves the water running during the task (data courtesy of the United States Geological Survey).

- Determine the monetary cost of supplying water to homes.
- Investigate the amount of water used for agriculture, mining, thermoelectric power, and industry in your community.
- Investigate which states have the greatest annual consumption of water.
- Calculate the amount of water consumed at home, and then develop a plan to reduce consumption by 10 percent.

Resources
The United States Geological Survey—*water.usgs. gov/watuse*. This website provides numerous resources for teachers and students regarding water related data and activities. Students can even find a *leak calculator* to help them determine the amount of water that can be lost over a given period of time.

Stephen J. Farenga is an associate professor of science education, Beverly A. Joyce is an associate professor of testing and measurement, and Daniel Ness is an assistant professor of mathematics education at Dowling College in Oakdale, New York.

Breaking the Code: Examining Your Mail

By Stephen J. Farenga, Beverly A. Joyce, and Daniel Ness

You might be astonished to learn that it is possible to determine the origin of a piece of mail by simply examining the zip code on the upper left-hand corner of the envelope. In fact, a postal employee can identify the destination of a letter to a friend, relative, or business by the five-digit zip code and four-digit extension (six-character postal code—three letters followed by three numbers—in Canada and Mexico).

Each number in a zip code informs us about something having to do with location. The left-most digit tells us the area or region of the United States a piece of mail is coming from or traveling to. For example, states whose first number of the zip code begins with "0" are Massachusetts, Rhode Island, New Hampshire, Maine, Vermont, Connecticut, New Jersey, and parts of New York. The number in the second place of the zip code refers to two things: the state where the piece of mail originated and the district or region of that state. The possibilities are narrowed even further by the third number that, along with the second digit, represents a region in a particular state, or perhaps a large

city. The fourth and fifth digits represent more specific areas, such as towns, villages, or regions within a large city. To identify the specific destination even more accurately, the postal service introduced the four-digit extension in 1983. The sixth and seventh numbers (the first two digits of the four-digit extension) refer to a delivery sector, which may be several blocks, a group of streets, a group of post office boxes, several office buildings, a single high-rise office building, a large apartment building, or a small geographic area. The last two numbers (the eighth and ninth numbers of the entire zip code) denote a delivery segment, which might be one floor of an office building, one side of a street between intersections, specific departments in a company, or a group of post office boxes.

Like area codes, zip codes are often changed due to urban expansion and rural regions that become suburbs. From a geopolitical perspective, the zip codes with the lowest numbers are in the New England region. The left-most digit increases southward toward Florida. From there, the numbers begin increasing northward

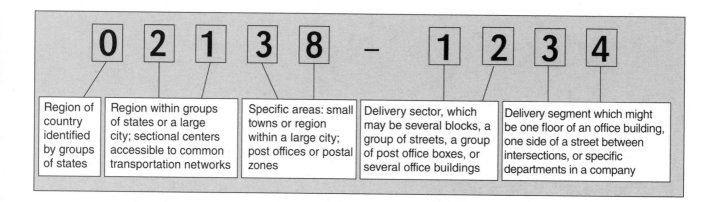

Breaking the Code

Objectives

Students will be able to use zip codes to identify local, national, and international geopolitical regions.

Materials

- U.S. or world maps
- pushpins with labels
- mail with a variety of addresses and zip codes
- index cards
- computer with internet access and spreadsheet program (optional)

Procedure

1. Keep a log of the mail that arrives at your home. A record will include at least three fields: city, state, and zip code. Additional fields, such as street address and personal names, are optional.
2. Place one record on each index card. It is important to keep one record per card so that cards may be sorted at a later time. Place the data into a spreadsheet or table. The information in the spreadsheet should contain the three fields listed above (city, state, zip code).
3. Locate each of the records on the map and place a pin on the spot with the corresponding zip code attached.
4. Examine the data on the map to identify any patterns between zip codes and geographic locations.
5. Using the spreadsheet or index cards, sort the data (i.e., zip codes) by either increasing or decreasing numerical values. Answer the following questions on a separate sheet of paper:
   - Do any patterns emerge in sorting the data?
   - Do any exceptions appear in the data?
   - How is the organization of zip codes similar to and different from scientific classification?
   - What do you think is the purpose of zip codes?
   - What other possible data or information can be obtained through the use of zip codes (e.g., population densities, census takers, geographic locations)?

and westward. For example, you will find 40202 in Louisville, Kentucky; 50309 in Des Moines, Iowa; 60601 in Chicago, Illinois; 75201 in Dallas, Texas; 80202 in Denver, Colorado; 92037 in La Jolla, California; 98101 in Seattle, Washington; and 99950 in Ketchikan, Alaska.

It is interesting to point out that, although the zip codes generally increase in number when traveling westward, some western zip codes are actually lower in number than many eastern zip codes. For example, although Des Moines, Iowa is due west of Chicago, Illinois, cities in Iowa have zip codes beginning with "5" while cities in Illinois have zip codes beginning with "6." Another case in point is the state of Montana. Although Montana is a western state, zip codes in that state begin with the numeral "5." Simply cross the border from Montana to Idaho and the first digit of the zip codes goes up to "8." Like all classification systems, there are always exceptions to the rules.

Classification

Carolus Linnaeus (1707–1778) developed a classification system that is the basis of our modern system in biology. The main classification groups are kingdom, phylum, class, order, family, genus, and species. The farther you move from the general (kingdom) to the specific (species), the more attributes a group of organisms has in common.

You can compare the modern classification

system of organisms to the mail system. First, the country to which the piece of mail is being sent must be identified (mostly by strings of characters, such as USA, CAN, and MEX), then, the correct state or province, then the right city or town, the proper street, the surname, and finally, the given name. Again, do you see how we move from the general to the specific?

In the included activity (see "Breaking The Code"), students will extend scientific thinking through the processes of classifying, observing, gathering, hypothesizing, and generalizing through the use of zip codes. The duration of this activity can vary from a couple of class periods to a long-term project that can span multiple marking periods. The zip-code map helps students learn local, national, and international geography. As an extension, students may be interested in locating the latitude, longitude, counties, time zones, and geographic areas covered by specific zip codes. They may even calculate the distance between zip codes and population densities within zip codes.

It is interesting to note the role technology plays in the development of classification systems. Organisms are no longer classified simply by structural similarities. Scientists may now use DNA to support the existence of relationships among organisms. Similarly, technology has also aided the postal system in the development of the expanded zip code from five to nine digits, and even 11-digit codes that more specifically identify geographic locations.

In every environment—home, work, or school—we are always classifying. Further, classification is more than merely a scientific or mathematical endeavor; it's a human endeavor. We do it even if we aren't realizing it. What makes classification with regard to zip codes a scientific endeavor is one's ability to observe, gather, hypothesize, organize, and generalize from the given data.

Stephen J. Farenga is an associate professor of science education, Beverly A. Joyce is an associate professor of testing and measurement, and Daniel Ness is an assistant professor of mathematics education at Dowling College in Oakdale, New York.

Internet

Zip code lookup

www.usps.com/zip4/welcome.htm Allows you to find the code for a particular location. In addition, you can identify all the zip codes for a city or town, or all the cities and towns within a particular zip code.

ZipInfo.com

www.zipinfo.com/search/zipcode.htm A commercial site that allows you to obtain county name, time zone, latitude, and longitude of a geographic area.

Postal information resources

www.refdesk.com/factpost.html Contains postal resources, the addresses to postal systems of other countries.

Get Familiar With Fingerprints

Fingerprints are made up of ridges in the skin that form lines of many different shapes and sizes. They are formed before you are born and never change throughout your life. Your fingerprint might contain an arch, a loop, a whorl, or a mixture of these. These three major patterns and their variations distinguish fingerprints into different types. In addition to the lines in a fingerprint that you can see, there are tiny patterns made up of distinct points between and at the end of fingerprint ridges, called minutiae. These points are what make each fingerprint truly unique.

Why Are Fingerprints Important?

In ancient times, fingerprints were used to seal important papers or business deals. It wasn't until hundreds of years later that fingerprints were discovered to be unique to individuals and to have many applicable uses. The most familiar use of fingerprints is to solve crimes. Whenever you touch something, you leave behind your fingerprint. If your hands are dirty, the fingerprints are visible.

Fingerprints that are not visible to the naked eye are called latent. They are produced by naturally occurring substances on the skin. Law enforcement officials have techniques for capturing latent fingerprints and making them visible.

No two fingerprints are alike—not even those of identical twins. Police classify fingerprints by their patterns. With the help of today's computers, the police can attempt to match fingerprints from a crime scene with more than 80 million fingerprints in their database.

Fingerprints can also be used in other ways. For example, using measurements of human characteristics for identification is called biometry. You may have seen fingerprints on a credit card or seen someone in a movie use their fingerprint to enter a high security area.

Now that you have learned a little about fingerprints, can you guess what type of fingerprint you have? Make a set of your own fingerprints and try classifying them into the different types.

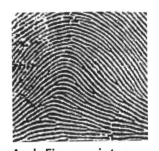

Arch Fingerprint

Loop Fingerprint

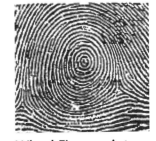

Whorl Fingerprint

Family Fingerprinting

Materials:
- One soft-leaded pencil
- Transparent tape

Time needed:
About 30 minutes

Directions:

1. Rub pencil lead on a piece of paper to create a 3 cm² "ink-pad."

2. Rub your finger pad onto the lead square, covering the entire pad area until the joint.

3. Press a piece of clear tape onto the leaded pad of your fingertip.

4. Lift off the tape—be careful not to touch the print—and place the tape onto its proper square on the graph below.

5. Have three friends or family members do the same.

6. Investigate the fingerprints and label each one "W" for whorl, "A" for arch, "L" for loop, or "M" for a mixture in the small box next to each fingerprint.

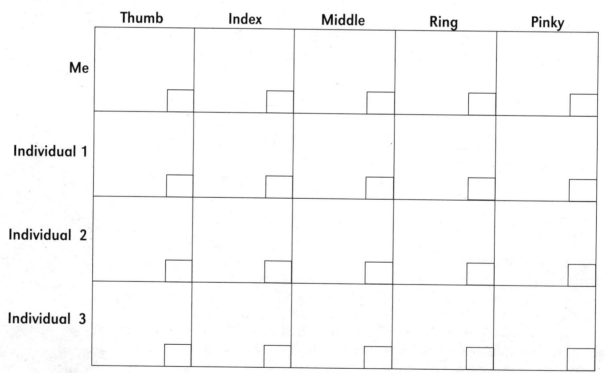

Questions:

1. What do you observe?

2. Who has loops, whorls, and arches?

3. Does anyone have a mixture?

4. What is the most common type of fingerprint in your group?

5. Can you find differences in the fingerprints that seem similar?

NATIONAL SCIENCE TEACHERS ASSOCIATION

Family Viewing

By Patrisha J. Bronzell

Although some people believe that contemporary TV offers few family-viewing opportunities, most educators agree that this medium can be a valuable educational tool with adult guidance. Programs on ecology, animal behavior, natural phenomena, and engineering wonders are regularly highlighted on PBS and educational cable channels. These science programs, when paired with internet connections, can make learning at home a reality.

But what if no specific homework assignment needs to be completed? Would a day of watching science programs shared between a parent and child be an enjoyable, rewarding, and no-pressure learning experience? My son Tysen and I found ourselves grappling with these very questions. Although my son was not given any science homework for the weekend, we decided to make our Saturday a day of learning. We checked the online listings for the Discovery Channel and The Learning Channel, and decided to watch a series on weather and the challenges and consequences of humankind attempting to control its environment.

The first program of our Saturday learning was titled "Wind: Heaven's Breath." When we tuned in, we saw a tumbleweed being blown across desert land and learned that the spines of the tumbleweed, or wind flower, can pierce leather. This got us thinking about how plants are designed to survive extreme conditions, and before long we were deep in discussion about the survival mechanisms of the saguaro cactus and the Venus flytrap. My son suggested that we look up these species on the internet after the show.

Turning our attention back to the program, we learned about the Santa Ana winds of Southern California, which are hot, dry winds that descend from the mountainous terrain. We learned that big cities such as Chicago experience winds that flow in a vertical *downwash*—a downward airstream—because of the many skyscrapers. The wind's momentum creates swirls and eddies powerful enough to sweep pedestrians off their feet. We also learned that buildings radiate heat that has a warming effect on the wind and creates a *microclimate* in the cities.

Before long, we both had questions that the program didn't answer, so we turned off the TV and set out to find our own answers. My son collected some reference books while I browsed Compton's Encyclopedia on CD-ROM. When I typed in the keyword *wind,* we discovered that there are two calm belts on either side of the equator called *horse latitudes.* Our internet search revealed that there are numerous types of winds, including the Philippine *gaguio* (a tropical cyclone wind), a French *mistral* (a strong, freezing wind that funnels down the Rhône Valley), and an Italian *tramontana* (a brisk, cool wind that blows southward from the Alps).

Wind was only the first topic in the TV series—hurricanes, floods, tornadoes, and global catastrophes soon followed. Unfortunately, we began to notice an emphasis on miraculous and incredible rescue attempts rather than on the science behind the various weather conditions; however, this in itself became a good topic for discussion. Still, we forged ahead, ready to learn all there was to know about weather.

Next, we discovered that hurricanes are formed in the Atlantic Ocean, typhoons are formed in the western Pacific Ocean, and cyclones are formed in the Indian Ocean. From the CNN website we downloaded hurricane facts and figures that included storm names, regions, and categories. There we found links to a storm-tracking system, or weather watch. We decided to bookmark this site for future reference.

While conducting our research, we noted that our print sources didn't always jibe with the information on the websites. I cautioned my son about taking what's printed as fact, for information becomes outdated, facts are not always verified, and typos often occur. As we discovered, websites can be inaccurate, so we consulted only those sites we considered reliable. Most of the discrepancies, however, had to do with wind measurements—we decided that how things are measured can lead to differences in measurement data.

By midafternoon we read about flash floods, tsunamis, thunder, and lightning, and we admitted to ourselves that our day of learning was jam-packed with too much information. We obviously did not become experts on any one topic, but that was not our objective. We wanted to see if viewing science-related programs was something we could do together. As a result, we discovered that we share a mutual curiosity of science that sparked an ongoing dialogue. And in the final analysis, dialogue is what it's all about.

The following day, we browsed several on-line booksellers, such as Amazon, Barnes and Noble, and Powell's Books, and logged on to our local library's online catalog. We each picked one topic to further investigate, and we set aside a day to swap our newfound information. It looks like we will be spending a lot more Saturdays learning science. We never did get back to finding out about saguaros and Venus flytraps, but I imagine we will at some point.

Patrisha J. Bronzell is a library specialist at Seely Place School in Scarsdale, New York.

Internet

CNN Weather
  http://weather.cnn.com/weatherforecast.jsp
Discovery Channel
  www.discovery.com
The Learning Channel
  www.tlc.com

Museums as Inquiry Role Models

By Stephen J. Farenga, Beverly A. Joyce, and Daniel Ness

One way to bridge the gap between informal and formal science is to broaden students' science contexts by taking them to museums. Parents often ask how they can take advantage of museums or science resource centers within their community. In actuality, they want to know how their children's attention can be focused on learning while visiting the museum. Science museums have a unique advantage over many classrooms in that they are stocked with rich resources. Museums generally include displays, hands-on activities, and the freedom to explore and learn at one's own pace. In addition, the museum experience may provide students with appropriate stimuli to generate questions that will further inquiry. Inquiry requires students to have background knowledge to frame appropriate questions for study. The issue is not just a matter of problem solving; rather, it's one of problem posing.

Observing People at the Museum

It is amazing what we can learn about parent and child interactions while observing them at museums. As museums place greater emphasis on high-tech exhibits, we are surprised to see children revert back to the traditional displays of the large mammals, birds, fish, and reptiles. When we ask students why they were interested in these exhibits, most state that "The most interesting animals are the ones that are extinct, and are the largest mammals," "We can't always see the animals that well at the zoo because they might not be out," "The animals at the museum aren't moving, so you can observe them longer," or "There were parts of the animal in the museum that you can see up close" (such as the size of the paws, claws, mouth, and teeth of bears). Upon further prodding, students indicate that they are able to observe all the characteristics of an organism (such as their size, shape, teeth, claws, and body segments).

On our continued visits to science museums, parents and children are often seen engaging in exhibit investigation and participating in hands-on activities. We notice that some parents seem comfortable guiding their children through the museum, enjoying and making the most of the informal science learning opportunities available. Other parents, however, could probably use some assistance. As teachers, we can provide parents with the inspiration, guidance, and necessary tools to add enjoyment, excitement, and adventure to family museum trips.

By preparing parents for museum visits, teachers can help create a field experience that can serve as a motivator for upcoming science units. Primarily, teachers need to convey to parents the techniques they practice every day in the classroom. Just as with a classroom lesson, a successful museum visit requires preparation, guidance during the lesson, and follow-up.

Preparation for Learning

Gathering an audience may not be as difficult as you think. Teachers can present workshops on helping parents or other group leaders make the most of museum visits by contacting their parent-teacher organizations. This provides teachers with the opportunity to increase communication between home and school, while at the same time promoting their science programs. One important way to prepare parents with the opportunities mentioned above is to provide them with an outline of the topics you plan to cover during the school year. Knowing the students' curriculum helps parents choose which museums to visit and gives them time to prepare for their visits. By linking informal learning with a curriculum topic, parents encourage students to make real-world connections. This makes seemingly abstract science concepts relevant and facilitates learning.

Another important means by which you can prepare parents is by sharing what you know about regional and national museums. Identify the museum's education specialist and ask about developmentally appropriate programs for students. Request educational materials that the museum provides about its programs, and prepare study guides tailored to your curriculum. In our experience working with parent groups, some feel apprehensive about teaching

Figure 1.
Making a museum plan.

Obtain a floor plan of the museum
The more detailed the plan is the better. If sufficient detail is not provided, try the internet, contact a museum resource person, or make a personal visit to determine which exhibits are displayed and how they are arranged. With the floor plan, you can explain the general layout of exhibits and the reason for their arrangements, but be aware that exceptions may be found for some classification systems due to new discoveries in science, divergent theories, outdated exhibits, or limited resources.

Systems, order, and organization
Have students determine a rule, pattern, or reason used to create the hall, exhibit, or display.

Examples
Living organisms may be arranged from cells, tissues, organs, organisms, populations, and communities. Physical systems may be arranged by the complexity of matter from particles, atoms, and molecules. Just as the solar system is arranged in a specific manner with the terrestrial planets closest to the Sun and gaseous planets farther away from the Sun.

their children science content. In addition, some state that the designs of most museums are too complex to investigate without a plan. Teachers can solve this problem by developing units of investigation or focus questions that recognize science as a human activity. A general museum guide for parents that provides questioning techniques or instructions for "walking" the museum can be effectively used with a little preparation. Figure 1 is a suggested visitation plan framework that we found helpful with parents. It incorporates the *National Science Education Standards*, including Content Standard A—Science as Inquiry; Content Standard F—Science in Personal and Social Perspectives; Content Standard G—History and Nature of Science; and Content Standard K–12, Unifying Concepts and Processes (NRC 1996).

Promoting Further Inquiry

Explain to parents how to convert their children's questions into a discovery process. Sending instructional guides home or conducting a workshop—such as the parent-teacher workshops mentioned above—for families outside of school could accomplish this. Parents should have students suggest answers to their own questions instead of providing them with a quick and easy answer. In another type of query, parents can ask questions that require the child to make careful observations, such as:

- What do all of the organisms in this hall or exhibit have in common?
- Is there any reason why the organisms are arranged or sequenced in a particular order?
- What is a good name for this exhibit?
- What does this remind you of?
- If you could create an exhibit, what would it be?

Responding to questions stimulates children's critical-thinking skills and fosters the development of other science-process skills,

Figure 2.
Critical-thinking prompts.

Foster or promote knowledge
(information identification and recall)
- What did you see at the science exhibit?
- Describe the science activity you completed.

Foster or promote comprehension
(ability to organize and select facts)
- What is the main point of the science exhibit?
- What is the main goal of the science activity?
- Explain the meaning of _____.

Foster or promote application skills
(use of facts, rules, and principles)
- Describe how A is related to B.
- Why is this fact, rule, or principle important?
- If this is done to X, what will happen to Y?

Foster or promote analytical skills
(understanding of relationships)
- How are the two exhibits the same?
- In what ways do the two exhibits differ?
- What are the elements of the science activity?
- What is the relationship of X to Y?

Foster or promote synthesis skills
(ability to join ideas together to form the big picture)
- What do you think would happen if _____?
- What would you include in a new science exhibit?
- Predict what would happen if you were to combine X with Y.
- Identify a solution for _____.

Foster or promote evaluation skills
(ability to form opinions, judgments, or decisions based on evidence)
- What criteria would you use to assess the exhibit?
- How would you decide about changing an exhibit?
- What do you think about _____?

such as comparing, identifying, describing, predicting, and summarizing (see Figure 2 for a guide to encouraging critical thinking).

Planning the Visit

Suggest to parents that they involve their children in planning the museum visit. Children who participate in planning and don't feel like they are being dragged to a museum against their will are often more apt to be engaged in learning. For example, children can perform a search on the internet at home or in the library to identify available museum programs, to find out the fees for various exhibits, and to determine hours of operation. If students are searching the internet, have them tell parents when they come across interesting resources. For example, some internet sites have online exhibits and science activities the family can examine before the trip to the museum. Additionally, museum staff can often answer science questions submitted via e-mail.

Lessons and teaching plans can also be accessed at most websites. In addition, students and parents who find it difficult to visit a museum in person may take a virtual tour of many interesting museum websites (see internet resources for examples). "Ology" means *the study of,* and on the American Museum of Natural History's website you can explore and learn about many interesting "ologies," including genetics, biodiversity, herpetology, ornithology, ichthyology, entomology, astronomy, archeology, and many others. Of course, these are not the only museum websites available. The Association of Science-Technology Centers Incorporated (ASTC) has more than 400 museum members located in the United States and around the world (see internet resources for additional websites on museum exhibits).

Museum Visit Follow-Up

Parents should encourage children to talk to their teachers, friends, and relatives about their adventure at the museum. Many of these museums even have afterschool and summer programs to further interest students. Asking children to describe the highlights of the experience, such as what they liked and what they discovered, reinforces what they learned during their visit.

Urge parents to investigate further opportunities for their children to pursue any newfound interests. For example, a child who especially enjoys a telescope exhibit could benefit from more encounters with related topics, such as going to the library, watching astronomy television shows, examining the night sky, or visiting websites for more information about planets and astronomy. Reinforcing budding interests may be the first step toward a career in science.

Invite students to share their museum experiences in the classroom. Guide them in finding connections to material covered in class. Group classmates together who have similar interests and guide each group to design their own activities.

The School-Museum Connection

Informal science learning environments can provide students with the opportunities to engage, explore, explain, elaborate, and evaluate topics related to science. Integrating formal experiences with informal science-related experiences may assist in increasing students' scientific literacy. The importance of linking informal experiences outside of school with formal instruction in school has been highlighted by the National Science Teachers Association (NSTA) in the 1998 *Informal Science Education Position Statement.* NSTA supports the development of associations between institutions of informal learning and schools as a way of meeting the goals stated in the *National Science Education Standards.* Teachers who are interested in investigating or forming collaborations with community-based learning environments may find the Museums and Public Schools Initiative (MAPS) website useful in developing a comprehensive education plan linking informal and formal learning (see internet resources).

Stephen J. Farenga is an associate professor of science education, Beverly A. Joyce is an associate professor of testing and measurement, and Daniel Ness is an assistant professor of mathematics education at Dowling College in Oakdale, New York.

References

National Research Council (NRC). 1996. *National Science Education Standards*. Washington DC: National Academy Press.

National Science Teachers Association (NSTA). 1998. *Informal Science Education Position Statement*. Available at *www.nsta.org*.

Internet

The American Museum of Natural History
www.amnh.org/ology
Exploratorium, San Francisco, California
www.exploratorium.edu
The Franklin Institute Science Museum, Philadelphia, Pennsylvania
www.fi.edu
The Computer Museum, Boston, Massachusetts
www.tcm.org
The Museum of Science and Industry, Chicago, Illinois
www.msichicago.org
Association of Science-Technology Centers Incorporated
www.astc.org
Museum of Paleontology at the University of California at Berkeley
www.ucmp.berkeley.edu/diapsids/dinosaur.html
Museums and Public Schools Initiative
www.museumsandpublicschools.org

Capitalizing on Student Travel in Earth Science Classrooms

By Andrew Gilbert

When I taught middle school, students who took extended vacations during the school year provided a recurring challenge for me. I had trouble coming up with meaningful lessons and activities that would engage these students during their time away from the classroom. Early in my career, I would simply assign readings and activities based on the textbook that students could complete in a car or airplane. However, I knew that I was not providing the student with the rich experiences that science has to offer. After much frustration, I devised a way of tying in their travels to the study of Earth science.

Traveling Geologic Investigators

Before the trip, ask the student to research the area he or she will be visiting. Have the student identify important geological features, familiarize himself or herself with the climate, and gather information about the biome being visited. This will generate student enthusiasm about the project and the trip itself.

Next, explain to the student that he or she will be collecting data during the trip that will be shared with the rest of the class when the student returns. This can include information on

- geological and topographical features,
- ways that humans alter the environment,
- utilization of Earth's resources, and
- efforts of conservation/preservation.

To supplement the data collected, encourage the student traveler to take a lot of pictures. If he or she doesn't have access to a camera, consider purchasing a disposable camera or loaning the student an inexpensive digital camera. Instruct the student to keep a photo journal in which he or she can provide information about each picture and explain how it relates to the study of Earth science.

When the student returns to the classroom and you have had a chance to review the information collected, work with the student to develop a research question related to his or her travels. For example:

- How do weathering and erosion influence the topography of Vietnam?
- How does Copper Canyon, located in northern Mexico, compare to the Grand Canyon of Arizona?
- How do you see the results of plate tectonics impacting the lives of the people within the country you visited?

Give the student a week or two to create a short report that addresses the research question. At the end of that time, the report is shared with the rest of the class as part of a presentation that includes a slide show or PowerPoint presentation of images from the trip.

The Travels of Max

To provide some details and possibilities of this approach, I want to share the travels of Max, a former student who spent five weeks visiting relatives in Argentina over winter break (he missed nearly three weeks of class time). Before he left, I spoke with Max and came up with some questions for him to research before his trip. These included:

- How large is Argentina?
- Where will you be traveling?
- What are some geologic features you will encounter?
- Give some examples of particular ways that the theory of plate tectonics and/or sea-floor spreading directly involves South America.

Next, I contacted Max's parents in a letter and by phone to explain the major points of the project and see if they had any suggestions for lessons or activities. They were delighted with the idea and informed me that they would be driving from Buenos Aires to the western edge of the country, so Max would be able to observe geologic features along the way.

A few days before Max left for his trip, he was issued a digital camera and I had him take some practice shots around the school grounds. I also provided him with a notebook to use as his photo journal. Lastly, we made a formal announcement to the class that Max would be traveling to Argentina to study geology and he would document his travels and observations to share with us upon his return. I was also able to align our classroom curriculum to focus on earthquakes and plate tectonics during Max's absence, with an emphasis on South America. In particular, we would study the subduction zone along the western coast.

While on his trip, Max took photos of geologic features and recorded related questions and observations in his photo journal. For example, when he was in the western part of Argentina and was able to view the Andes, he noted that he was struck by their size and beauty.

Upon his return, we discussed the trip and possible research questions. We eventually decided that he would research the formation of the Andes mountain range and their relationship to the "ring of fire." This research question was incorporated into his slide presentation, which he shared with the class a few weeks after he returned.

Challenges of This Approach

It is important to remember that this project is open-ended and individualized for a particular student on a particular trip. The context of the trip can change depending on the country, the student, economic position of the family, and so on. It is important to understand that some students may be visiting only cities or may be unable to travel once arriving at their destination. For example, when my student Liza visited Baranquilla, Columbia, her family had no plans to travel outside the city. Consequently, she chose to document how geologic features affected people's everyday lives in a city. The goal was to show how humans adapt to their environment and how they adapt their environment to their lives.

Liza's trip illustrates one of the chief challenges of this project approach, which is how to best connect with parents and let them understand they are not obligated to do anything special for the project. I do not want to burden parents, especially ones with limited means, by requiring that they take their children on a special excursion. Often, however, sightseeing is part of the itinerary anyway, so special side trips don't need to be worked into the trip.

Teaching students to take good photos and make detailed observations is another challenge of this project. Most students are not familiar with lighting, composition, and other key features of photography. And most are probably unaccustomed to making field notes while on vacation. As suggested earlier, allowing students to practice with a digital camera on school grounds beforehand can improve the quality of student images. You can also have them practice writing descriptions of images in magazines such as *National Geographic* to try to improve their descriptive-writing skills.

Successes of This approach

In the course of just a few years in an urban middle school setting, I had students make presentations on trips to Mexico, Guatemala, Honduras, Argentina, Columbia, Kenya, Vietnam, and Kazakhstan. These trips provided my entire class with a glimpse of the world and instilled in them the idea that the world is a large and diverse place. Furthermore, it provided several chances to integrate with other subjects, particularly social studies. Some of the projects designed in conjunction with social studies included the following topics:

- colonization and history
- economics and globalization
- cultures and customs of other countries

Often the students who were the most successful with this project were the students whom I struggled to motivate in my classroom on a daily basis. In the case of Liza, for example, it was difficult to get her interested in Earth science and I often could not get her to engage in lab and class activities. She was excited about this project, however, and turned in a nice photo journal with good supporting notes and observations. She also turned in her written research report on beach dynamics.

These travel projects not only generate interest in Earth science, but they also foster in students a deeper understanding and appreciation of the places they visit. They also provide parents with an additional avenue to teach their children and learn along with them.

Finally, the research paper aspect of the project helps teachers align these activities with specific concepts tied to state and national content standards. Students have a vested interest in learning about these concepts now that they have witnessed them in the field. This approach also allows teachers to drive home the standards that relate to the process of science—collecting data, hypothesizing, asking questions, communicating results, and so on. All in all, this project approach enables teachers to engage students in a way that is not possible with the textbook-driven readings or worksheets that are often given when students miss large blocks of class time.

Andrew Gilbert is an assistant professor in the Department of Teaching Leadership and Curriculum Studies at Kent State University in Kent, Ohio.

Resources

Baptiste, P., and S. Key. 1996. Cultural inclusion. *The Science Teacher* 63 (2): 33–35.

Fusco, D., and A. Calabrese-Barton. 2001. Representing student achievements in science. *Journal of Research in Science Teaching* 38 (3): 337–54.

Ladson-Billings, G. 1994. *The dreamkeepers: Successful teachers of African American children.* San Francisco, CA: Jossey-Bass.

Leavell, A., M. Cowart, and R. Wilhelm. 1999. Strategies for culturally responsive teachers. *Equity and Excellence in Education* 32 (1): 64–71.

National Research Council (NRC). 1996. *National Science Education Standards.* Washington, DC: National Academy Press.

———. 2000. *Inquiry and the national standards: A guide for teaching and learning.* Washington, DC: National Academy Press.

Section 5

Informal Institutions: Museums, Zoos, and Other Field Trips

Informal Institutions

Museums, Zoos, and Other Field Trips

Informal learning is defined as voluntary learning that takes place outside of the traditional classroom environment. As John Falk (2002) reports, "Research suggests that nearly half of the public's understanding of science derives from [the informal and free-choice learning] sector, which supports the ongoing and continuous learning of all citizens." The power of museums, zoos, and other informal centers is clear. In a summary of the research. Colin Johnson offers the following analysis.

There is strong evidence that:

- Museums and science centers provide motivating and enriching environments for learning. Immediate impact can be exciting, but the "slow burn" effects on learning and motivation are more significant.
- This "free-choice" environment strongly engages the attention of learners and allows for responses in relation to their individual backgrounds.
- Museums and science centers also support the educational role of parents and teachers.

- An important opportunity provided by science centers concerns "talking to learn." Conversation, whether with family members or peer groups leads to that articulation of ideas which is at the heart of assimilating them. Such social learning opportunities cannot readily be achieved in schools.
- Learning in museums and science centers takes place in a wider world context which begins with the learner's prior experience, takes in the interactive opportunities and—very importantly—the related programming activities provided by the center. Teachers as well as students learn from this process.
- Science centers provide venues for discussion, consultation, and deliberation which are widely perceived as neutral—in relation to political adherence and even in relation to the scientific community as a whole....

When you are making plans and identifying purposes for a visit to an informal science center, you must take many considerations into account. Children begin a field trip with two agendas. The first focuses on what students visualize doing—seeing exhibits, having fun traveling to the site, buying items at the gift shop, and having a day away from the norms of school. The second agenda comes from the expectations set by the school and museum: This agenda is that they will learn things and be able to meet people who work at the museum. The interplay of the students' agendas has an impact on the outcomes of the trips. (Falk and Dierking 1992). Not all teachers have the same ideas in mind. Some view the field trip as a change of pace for students and a social experience. Some have learning-oriented goals. Griffin (1998) found that teachers' explicit and implicit purposes may differ. They might say that the trip should be enriching and social but then provide students with a series of worksheets. The lesson to be learned is that expectations must be based on real expectations that are carefully crafted, clear, and communicated to everyone involved in the experience.

In This Section (articles are in italics)

This section begins with a series of articles providing tips on how to prepare for a trip to an informal learning center.

The first, *Have a Safe Trip,* provides guidelines for a safe trip and includes a bulleted list of important considerations for any trip away from school grounds.

More Than Just a Day Away From School is a step-by-step guide in planning a successful field trip. This guide is appropriate for any local off-campus site to which you may travel and includes all aspects from setting goals to designing activities.

If you are interested in planning a longer trip, you'll want to read *How to Plan, Survive, and Even Enjoy an Overnight Field Trip With 200 Students.* This guide provides valuable guidance in every aspect of planning including setting the purpose; fund-raising; establishing rules of conduct; securing transportation, lodging, and food; chaperones; trip activities; and follow-up after the trip.

The final three articles focus on specific informal sites and what they offer for students and teachers. This section will provide a wealth of models to serve as beginning points in your thinking and planning as you tap your own resources, even though you may not find a site in your area with the specific features of these sites

The Wrap on Raptors provides an overview of a student field trip to an avian conservation facility, one of several raptor observatories in the United States.

Welcome to the Congo is a look through the lens of a teacher participating in professional development workshops at the Bronx Zoo. These two articles provide evidence of the types of experiences available to teachers and students through informal sites.

We certainly don't all have Yellowstone National Park in our area. But, *Hot Spot at Yellowstone* can provide insight to the type of activities students (and adults) may participate in while visiting. This article also provides links to electronic field trips—making a trip through Yellowstone possible even if it isn't in your neighborhood.

Websites for informal science institutions provide a rich array of teaching guides, lessons, field trip ideas, virtual field trips, and resources. Many of the ideas are not limited to use at the specific site and are easily adapted for use at related facilities or off site. In addition you will find pages for school groups, camps, clubs, and scouts at many of these sites.

Visit the website of your local informal institution for more information concerning their programs. You will also find floor plans and current exhibit information that are valuable in your planning. Here are some of the well-known institutions:

- Adler Planetarium—*www.adlerplanetarium.org*
- American Museum of Natural History—*www.amnh.org*
- The Bronx Zoo—*www.bronxzoo.com*
- The Exploratorium—*www.exploratorium.edu*
- Florida Museum of Natural History—*www.flmnh.ufl.edu*
- The Fort Worth Museum of Science and History—*www.fwmuseum.org*
- The Franklin Institute Science Museum—*www.fi.edu*
- National Aquarium in Baltimore—*www.aqua.org*
- Natural History Museum of Los Angeles County—*www.nhm.org*
- National Optical Astronomy Observatory—*www.noao.edu*
- National Park Service—*www.nps.gov*
- San Diego Zoo and Wild Animal Park—*www.sandiegozoo.org*
- Sea World—*www.seaworld.org*
- Six Flags Theme Parks—*www.sixflags.com*
- The Smithsonian Institution—*www.si.edu*

References

Falk, J. H. 2002. The contribution of free-choice learning to public understanding of science. *Interciencia* 27 (2): 62–65.

Falk, J. H., and L. D. Dierking. 1992. *The museum experience*. Washington, DC: Whalesback books.

Griffin, J. 1998. *School-museum integrated learning experiences in science: A learning journey*. Unpublished doctoral dissertation.

Johnson, Colin. *Science centers as learning environments*. ASTC Resource Center. *www.astc.org/resource/education/johnson_scicenters.htm*.

National Science Teachers Association (NSTA). 1999. NSTA position statement on informal science education. Arlington, VA: NSTA. *www.nsta.org/about/positions.aspx*.

Resources

The articles listed are available through the Learning Center on the NSTA website at *http://learning-center.nsta.org*.

Easley, L. 2005. Cemeteries as science labs. *Science Scope* 29: 28–32.

Fredricks, A. D., and J. Childers. 2004. A day at the beach, anyone? *Science and Children* Summer: 33–37.

Melber, L. M. 2000. *Tap into informal science learning*. *Science Scope* 23: 28–31.

National Research Council (NRC). 1996. *National Science Education Standards*. Washington, DC: National Academy Press.

Summers, S. 2004. Museums as resources for science teachers. *Science Scope* Summer: 28–29.

Yager, R. E. and J. Falk. 2008. *Exemplary Science in informal education settings: Standards-based success stories*. Arlington, VA: NSTA Press.

Have a Safe Trip!

By Juliana Texley

Relativity isn't just a science term. It sometimes guides our judgments in science education too. Every day, in every lesson, we make decisions about safety relative to the maturity and knowledge base of our students and the environment in which we teach.

Science safety isn't just a set of rules. It requires common sense and that teacher intuition that helps us predict what might happen when we least expect it. To foster inquiry in a safe environment, middle school teachers must not only keep up to date with the latest information about products, hazards, and best practice, but also consider the developmental level of their budding scientists.

Open the Door to New Ideas

If you're contemplating an overnight field trip, the first thing to realize is that it needs careful planning if it is to be successful. That's good advice for shorter excursions too.

Every good field trip requires extra adult help. The number of chaperones isn't set by a formula; it depends upon where you are going, how much you'll expect of your students, and whether special-needs students will be included. Preplanning should take place with your chaperones. Unprepared adults can be less than helpful. And the chaperones should never be distracted by the presence of their own children on the trip.

Many field trips involve field studies, like rock collecting or pond analysis. Visit your site in advance. Use your special "teacher eyes" to try to anticipate the worst that might happen. Is there something that shouldn't be climbed but might be, such as a high-tension wire? Is there water, poison ivy, polluted water? Do you have permission to use all the property areas you need?

Don't Leave Home Without

Packing light is probably not the best advice for school field trips. As you leave the support of your institution, you'll be principal, teacher, and guide. You'll enjoy that trip all the more knowing you've taken every precaution for safety. Here are a few essentials:

- Reviewing your board of education's field trip policy.
- Information about your students' medical needs, allergies, and contact information. You must know about special needs and have written permission to obtain help for your students if the worst takes place.
- Directions and material safety data sheets. If your trip involves use of laboratory chemicals of any kind, you must bring both along. Take only the minimum in a locked container. (In general, whenever you can avoid carrying test chemicals on

a field trip, leave them at home. Also, instead of using chemicals in the field to perform tests, use portable probes.

- A cell phone or two-way, long-range walkie-talkie that will keep you in touch with the school. You'll need it for emergencies and to let the school know when you'll be arriving back so that parents can meet you.
- Appropriate dress and repellents for insects. West Nile and other insect-borne diseases are serious threats in many areas now. Make sure that you've informed parents in advance about the use of repellents, so that potential allergic reactions can be avoided.
- Behavior contracts with consequences that everyone understands and supports.

And Don't Bring

- Siblings or friends—other children who will not be subject to the rules you have set up.
- Student cell phones, extra games, very loud audio equipment, or materials that could distract or be stolen.

Juliana Texley, a science teacher and administrator with many years of experience, is a coauthor of the NSTA Press publications Exploring Safely: A Guide for Elementary Teachers; Inquiring Safely: A Guide for Middle School Teachers; Investigating Safely: A Guide for High School Teachers; *and* Science Safety in the Community College.

More Than Just a Day Away From School

By Michelle Scribner-Maclean and Lesley Kennedy

With all the things that middle school science teachers have to juggle during the year, designing a science field trip can seem like a daunting task. Fortunately, there are many strategies teachers can use to help ensure that field trips are more than just a day away from school—that they are instead a truly meaningful learning experience.

Some middle school science teachers have had students do scavenger hunts around museums and science centers. These experiences do not always engage student minds, however, or connect well to the science that students are learning at school or at home. Instead of simply handing students worksheets of things to locate in a science center, many teachers have found that, with a clear goal and some help from the staff at the field-trip site, they can plan science field trips that support their classroom teaching and get students excited about learning science.

What Research Has Taught Us About Field Trips

Researchers have been examining the elements of effective science field trips for decades. Wolins, Jensen, and Ulzheimer (1992) found that students tended to remember trips in which they had high involvement (mental engagement and actual physical engagement with exhibits and objects). Another factor in the success of field trips was whether or not the teacher built links into the curriculum. Researchers concluded that the strength of the field-trip experience was clearly affected by whether or not the teacher was able to create a context for the field trip.

Set Clear Goals

As with any successful learning experience, you should decide what the goals are for your science field-trip experience and communicate these goals to your students. Are you hoping that they will visit an exhibit that will reinforce the content you've been teaching in class in an in-depth manner? Are you hoping that they practice science-process skills in a variety of exhibits? Do you want them to gain an understanding of how technology can be integrated with science and engineering? In addition to content or skills-based goals, you might consider goals such as having students develop a positive attitude about science. Getting students excited about science is something that museums can do very well. Regardless of the goals for your trip, a clear focus will help you build the experience you want students to have while out of the classroom.

Before the field trip, you should plan to visit the site to become familiar with offerings and to help establish goals (Koran and Baker 1978).

Many science museums offer pretrip planning meetings to allow teachers to get an advanced peek at exhibits and resources available for students. Museum educators can often help teachers tailor their field-trip experience to the needs of their students. If a pretrip visit is not possible, many institutions will help teachers with remote planning through e-mail or phone conversations. In addition, there are several museums across the country with excellent websites for field-trip planning (see Resources). These resources can be used by teachers who are in rural areas, whose classes cannot afford the expense of a trip, or where taking students out of school would be disruptive to other teachers' classes. Figure 1 outlines some important questions a teacher should consider when planning a science field trip.

Figure 1.
Science field-trip planning questions.

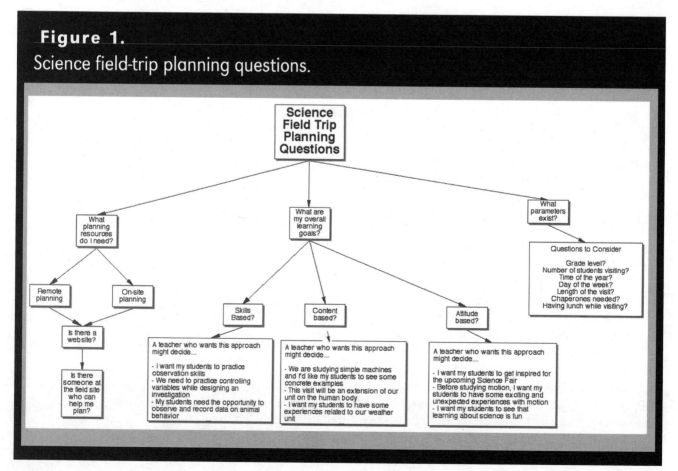

Figure 2.
Field-trip types and examples.

Field-trip type	Elements of this type of field trip	Examples
Open-ended experiences	• Addresses broad goals • These experiences can directly support developing a positive attitude about science and an excitement about learning science • Adaptable to many situations • Students can work individually or in groups • Can be created to ensure a highly interactive experience • Encourages students to make their own connections to the learning experiences	• Teacher-prepared trip sheets can be open-ended to guide inquiry and incorporate drawing, role-playing, and writing (Wolins, Jensen, and Ulzheimer 1992). • Free choice: Giving groups of students the opportunity to self-direct their science field-trip experience (Wolins, Jensen, and Ulzheimer 1992).
Focused experiences	• Addresses content or skill-specific goals • Asks students to concentrate on collecting specific type of data, but can also be adaptable to many situations • Students can work individually or in groups • Can be created to ensure highly interactive experience	• Lecture tours by museum educators • Teacher-prepared trip sheets use questions and hints that are completed by students during trip (Wolins, Jensen, and Ulzheimer 1992). See example in sidebar on p. 152. • Participatory lessons and presentations: In many science museums, teachers can choose from a set menu of classes that feature a variety of topics for different grade levels, which students attend as part of their field-trip visit.

Science Field-Trip Models: What Will Your Approach Be?

Museums provide many resources to help plan your science field-trip experience. Wolins, Jensen, and Ulzheimer (1992) found that teachers choose a variety of formats to structure student visits to museums. Some may find that they want students to have a more open-ended experience during their field trip, while others might choose for their students to have a more focused experience. Figure 2 explores the elements of these different field-trip types. Field-trip planners many intentionally incorporate some aspects of each type.

More Tools

In addition to the tools mentioned in this article, you might also decide to provide your students with digital cameras, clipboards, or digital video recorders to have them document what they learned. Regardless of your approach, with clear goals and some easy tools, science

Focusing your science field trip

Having a clear focus for your trip can have a positive impact on the experience for students (Bailey 1999). If you're trying to build a science field-trip experience that looks beyond the traditional scavenger hunt, you may want to design focus sheets for your middle school science students. A focus sheet looks dramatically different than the classic text-based scavenger hunt with 50 or so fill-in-the-blank questions, whose answers require little thought.

Here are some criteria to consider when designing your focus sheet:
- Be clear about your learning objective for the field trip.
- Articulate the trip goals to students.
- Create open-ended types of questions that require participants to interact with an exhibit or an exhibit component in pursuit of a response.
- Ask students to complete tasks that are appropriate for the learner's age and developmental level. Devise tasks that can realistically be accomplished in the busy museum setting.

Some things to keep in mind:
- Worksheets do not necessarily have to be completed by each individual. It can work well to have a group collectively respond to a challenge on one worksheet.
- While worksheets can help students understand what is expected of them during the field trip, worksheets may also limit free-choice learning opportunities unique to the science field-trip setting.
- Worksheets that require students to use one specific exhibit component may be difficult to complete because on any given day that component may be in high demand, under repair, or removed from the floor.
- Worksheets designed in any given year, based on specific exhibits, should always be revised because the exhibit halls change dramatically season to season and year to year.

Focus sheet
- At the field-trip site: Imagine that you have been sent by your local newspaper to review the exhibit.
- On a piece of paper: Write at least six comments about the exhibit (positive or negative) that will be the basis for your written review.
- Back in the classroom: Write a review of the exhibit. What was it about? What did you like or dislike? Who might be a good audience for this exhibit? What did you learn?

Animal observation
This activity can also be used by individual students or by a group. Although this particular example focuses on an observation of a tamarin, this activity could be modified to help students focus on the behavior of a variety of animals.

Tamarin observation sheet
- Observe all the tamarins for three to four minutes before collecting data. Be certain you understand each target behavior.
- Choose one tamarin to follow for five minutes. Note the behaviors on your sheet (see Figure 3).

Michelle Scribner-MacLean *is a visiting assistant professor at the University of Massachusetts Lowell Graduate School of Education in Lowell, Massachusetts.* Lesley Kennedy *is a teacher educator at the Museum of Science, Boston, with more than 20 years of experience helping teachers plan field trips.*

teachers can plan a meaningful and interesting science field-trip experience that can easily extend back into the classroom.

Sample Focused Field-Trip Activities

Everyone's a critic
This approach can be used by individuals or groups. The objective is for learners to experience an exhibit. The teacher may assign a given exhibit or involve students in choosing an exhibit.

References
Bailey, E. 1999. *School group visits to museums.* Available at *www.astc.org/resource/education/bailey.htm.*

Koran, J., and S. Baker. 1978. Evaluating the effectiveness of field experiences. In *What research says to the science teacher, Vol. 2,* ed. M. Rowe, pp. 50–64. Washington, DC: National Science Teachers Association.

Figure 3.
Tamarin observation.

Target behavior	Minute 1	Minute 2	Minute 3	Minute 4	Minute 5
Chasing					
Scent marking					
Eating (left or right hand?)					
Grooming (self or other)					
Additional behaviors noted					

Wolins, I., N. Jensen, and R. Ulzheimer. 1992. Children's memories of museum field trips: A qualitative study. *Journal of Museum Education* 17 (2): 17–27.

Resources
Boston Museum of Science
www.mos.org/educators. This website provides a wide variety of teacher tools for field-trip planning, including exhibits and programs mapped to curriculum frameworks and national standards.

Exploratorium (San Francisco)
www.exploratorium.edu/educate/index.html.

Fort Worth Museum of Science and History
www.fwmuseum.org/educate/field_trips_omni.html.

Monterey Bay Aquarium
www.mbayaq.org/lc/teachers_place/fieldtrip.asp.

How to Plan, Survive, and Even Enjoy an Overnight Field Trip With 200 Students

by Valarie Giacalone

"**A**re you serious?" "You'll regret this." "It will never work." These were just some of the comments I received from fellow teachers, parents, and friends when they first heard that I was planning a trip to Yellowstone National Park for my entire group of 196 eighth graders. Several years and several trips later, here are a few things I have learned from planning these field trip extravaganzas.

Preparation Is Necessary

Have a legitimate purpose. You will have to justify the time, expense, and value of this trip to fellow teachers, administrators, and parents, so you need to make it connect to your curriculum in obvious ways. Our first trip began when I discovered that most of my rural students had never been to Yellowstone, a mere four hours away. Your own trip would depend on your curriculum, resources, students, and interests. Good ideas for trips can come from fellow teachers, museums, state universities, and the internet.

After investigating commercial trip packages, it became apparent that the only way to afford a trip was to plan it all ourselves. It turned out that this was to our benefit, as it allowed us to tailor the trip to our specific needs. We tie almost every element of our yearly science curriculum to the destination. We study geology, volcanoes, earthquakes, glaciers, erosion, food webs, ecosystems, succession, microbiology, chemical reactions, rocks and minerals, heat and energy transfer, animal life, climate, force and motion, and the scientific method in the context of Yellowstone. We make a field book to guide our study while on the trip, which I score the same as a unit test. The field book contains information and questions to keep students focused during the trip. It has plant keys, animal track keys, scavenger hunt questions, Yellowstone facts, an animal-spotting log, thermal feature comparison pages, trail maps, questions for each stop, travel guides for times between stops, and blank journal pages to draw and describe features. Activities in the book include answering questions, drawing sketches, describing sights, and answering "why" questions. The students are guided by their field books. It is very student-directed work, and mostly they work together to get the answers. The students are required to have the field book with them always, so there is something to guide them at every stop and during the drives in between.

This approach supports the National Science Education Standards' (NRC 1996) recommendation to nurture a community of learners and get students to accept responsibility for their own learning while fostering collaboration. Our curriculum, designed completely around Yellowstone, creates a setting for student work that is consistent with this Standards' recommendation. Also, the curriculum identifies and uses resources outside of the school.

Know the rules. The first step was talking to my principal and seeing if this kind of an activity was even feasible (see Figure 1). Although he was supportive of the idea, he could not believe I was thinking of taking *all* of my students. He shook his head, wished me luck and made sure that I knew the school had no money for field trips, and we would be responsible for funding the whole thing. He gave me a copy of the district guidelines, which stated the trip must be approved by our own on-site committee, the school board, and the superintendent of schools. The paperwork is substantial. There are proposals for committee approval, permission slips, medical forms, memos to parents, gear lists, and itineraries. These forms and memos will vary depending on your destination and the requirements of your

school and school district, but be sure to get started on them early and to keep duplicate copies of all important papers. In my case, keeping track of the money requires a duplicate receipt book (for parents), a ledger (for the district), and a spreadsheet (for me). Generally, all funds must be overseen by your school. I do not ask parent volunteers for help because I like to keep close tabs on the planning myself.

Figure 1.
Planning steps.

- Principal approval
- Proposal preparation
- On-site committee approval
- School board approval
- Hotel and bus reservations
- Total cost estimate
- Information letter to parents
- Permission/medical concern slips
- Research fund-raising ideas
- Fund-raisers
- Trip itinerary in detail
- Trip attendance requirements
- Final "who goes" list
- Field books
- Group signups
- Bus sign-ups
- Chaperones
- Movie vote
- Gearing list to parents
- Specific itinerary to parents
- Calling to warn restaurants
- Practicing accepted behaviors
- Last-minute trip review and expectations

Funding. Start early! We start eight months before the trip. We spend numerous class hours discussing fund-raising ideas, ranging from car washes to dances to a drop-off child-care night. In our area, the best fund-raisers have included drop-off a childcare night ($5 per child from 6 to 10 p.m. at the school). We advertise at elementary schools in our district. Parents drop kids off, and students watch the children who are divided into age groups. Pizza sales are also good for our area. Money from child-care night is divided among those who participate. The funds raised by individuals go into their own accounts (each student has one). That way, those who want to work the fund-raisers benefit, and those that don't care to, find another means. About half the kids choose to participate. Because of these efforts, not one student is left behind because of money. Those who are still short of the needed funds are invited out to my farm to clean pastures. Teens get very creative in finding ways to earn money if the alternative is shoveling manure.

Transportation. Research several different options. In our case, commercial buses are cheaper than school buses. The drivers come with the buses, and we take four large buses for our group of about 200. Other transportation could be school buses or district vans. Special driver's licenses are needed to transport students, and there may be district regulations on how far your school buses are allowed to travel. Due to insurance liabilities we use professional drivers. Transportation has proven to be the biggest expense, but students are as excited about riding in big buses with tinted windows, VCRs, and bathrooms as they are about going on the trip itself. We vote on which movies to watch on the trip (rated PG of course). In addition to videos, students do karaoke and animal spotting, there are field book guidelines and travel guides for each section of driving, and there is a lot of hanging around and talking.

Lodging. Again, research several options and always ask about group rates. You will find different options depending on where you plan to go. When I first contacted the hotels in West Yellowstone, many of them replied that they were "not interested" in having our group. But I finally found one that said they would love to have us and gave a great group rate. We put the girls on one floor and the boys on another. Because our trip is three days long, we like to mix up the accommodations. For the second night, we stay in cabins, arranged through the park's group reservations service. It is a good mix of civilization (heated pool and cable TV) one night, and rustic living (community bathrooms, cabins, and invented entertainment) the next.

Food. You can save a great deal of planning time and money by giving students free reign with their meals. We began by planning for catered group meals. These easily doubled the price of our trip, and no one could agree on a menu. So, we decided instead to have a meal free time. The students carry their own food money (about $50 each). I also carry about $500 in $5 bills for emergencies. Only one person has ever lost his money. We stop at spots that have food options ranging from convenience stores and fast food to nice restaurants and give students a certain amount of time to eat. The students love being able to decide what and where to eat on their own but are never far enough away that they can't be collected easily.

Group assignments. The students choose their own roommates in a four-to-a-room plan. Those who don't have preferences sign up as singles and I group them together. We then vote to decide which three groups of roommates will join up to form a chaperone group. Then we vote for which four chaperone groups will ride in a bus together. This voting system creates a sense of unity among the groups. Although the students get to vote for groups, chaperones, and buses, the final say is always mine, with no whining allowed. Girls are assigned female chaperones, and boys are assigned male chaperones. Parent chaperones always monitor their own kids.

Plan for free time. I don't like to allow a lot of free time on the trip. Tight scheduling prevents the large group of 14-year-olds from becoming too inventive with their free time. The night in town we have swimming or board games at the hotel and the night in the cabins we have water fights and stargazing, but mostly we hang out and talk.

Student helpers. In the past, a lifesaver for me has been to take along a handful of students from the previous year's trip who lead the hikes, do sweeps of the trails for stragglers, help students with their field books, patrol the halls at night to enforce curfew, and be extra eyes and ears for me. Young legs and the ability to function on no sleep are definitely advantageous in this situation.

Chaperones. We have teachers and parents volunteer for the trip, with one chaperone for every 12 students. Chaperones pay a token amount (usually $40). The rest is made up from free rooms (one per 20 booked) and student trip monies. Their duties are to count noses, make sure students get up on time, get tucked in at curfew, make it back to the bus after every stop, and stay safe. I handle all the discipline.

Discipline. This is always the big question on everyone's mind—how can I control a group this big? The truth is that they manage themselves. I talk very openly with them about how people say we teachers are crazy for even trying to take trips like this and that the students will let us down. Middle schoolers will rise to most challenges given them, and I make sure the students get caught up in this attitude. It becomes a personal mission for them to prove the doubters wrong.

Before we go, I set up a behavior contract, listing rules for the trip (see Figure 2). "No leaving the room between 9:30 p.m. and 6:30 a.m." "Treat teachers, chaperones, and fellow students with respect." "Be polite to everyone we meet." "Stay on the boardwalk!" "Be positive. Work hard." Each student and his or her parents sign the contracts. The students agree to obey the rules, and the parents agree to drive to the park and pick them up any time day or night if they break the rules. The threat of an angry mom driving four hours to pick up a disobedient child is far more effective than any discipline method I could come up with.

We also practice the behavior I expect of them in class before the trip. We practice ordering in restaurants, eating in public, tipping

Figure 2.
Behavior contract.

I agree to stay with my chaperones at all times and follow their directions.

I agree to be respectful to the teachers, staff (including park and hotel), and my fellow students.

I agree to respect the property of the bus, hotel, and park (do not litter or disturb vegetation or animals, or damage the rooms).

I agree to have a positive attitude, work hard, and learn a great deal.

I agree to follow all instructions and safety guidelines of Yellowstone Park, the bus and the hotel.

I agree to stay in my room between the curfew hours of 9:30 p.m. and 6:30 a.m.

I agree to stay on all walkways and paths.

I will NOT wander off these walkways and paths. It could result in severe accident or death.

I will NOT approach any wildlife for any reason.

I will NOT feed any wildlife—they can bite.

I will NOT leave my group without permission from my chaperone.

I understand that if I do not follow the above rules, I must go home IMMEDIATELY.

Student signature

I understand that if my child does not follow the above rules, I will be responsible for coming and getting him/her immediately.

Parent signature

On the Trip

Expect enthusiasm in the strangest places. When the outfitted buses pull up in front of the school, the students erupt into a roar of excitement. I shake my head—excited over buses? And what's the next thing they get excited about? The tiny microwaves and refrigerators in the hotel rooms. I have learned to expect victory dances from the students when a tree is correctly identified using their identification keys, and cheers when they find their first elk hoof print. Keep your expectations positive. Every year I am appalled at our first stop inside the park. My classes invariably take up the entire boardwalk, talk noisily, are unfocused, and almost force other people off the trail. It seems that transferring good behavior theory into real life is difficult. When the students complete the trail loop, we have our first chat about my expectations for their behavior. I explain that the rude and obtrusive behavior will stop or the buses will turn around and go home—it is their choice. They know I am serious, and at our next stop they practically fall over themselves being polite to other people. I hear cheery voices ringing out "Hi there! Nice day! Have a good trip!"

After that initial chat, literally every place we go complete strangers come up to me and comment, "What an incredible group of students! How are you getting them to behave? We've never seen students this polite before." Once I was moved to tears when an elegant, elderly Japanese gentleman approached me while I had the group gathered around me on the lawn. "I have traveled all over the world," he said, "and I have never seen a group of teenagers this well groomed, polite, and well behaved. You should be very proud of them." He bowed, and applauded my students. I cried openly, and even my tough guys got misty eyed.

Expect the unexpected. Be prepared for sick, sad, scared, wet, cold, hungry, homesick, giggly, tired, heartbroken, and hyperactive students. We have a paramedic along as a chaperone, carrying a big first aid kit. Although our school counselor is also a paramedic, there is usually a parent who volunteers who is a nurse, doctor, policeman, or emergency medical technician. We have medical forms on each child listing any potential problems and medication needs. Our permission slips have an "okay to treat" section that is signed by the parents. The kids carry their own medications and are in charge of them. We have cell phones in case of emergency and radios to keep track of each other. We have spare water, munchies, bandages, hats, lip balm, and cash. Two chaperones shadow our explorations in a pickup truck (a chaperone volunteers to drive his or her own vehicle and shadow the bus; we pay for gas) that we use for sprained ankles or wounded pride.

Enjoy yourself and your students. Once, when we were hiking cross-country to Old Faithful, I ran into a group of my students who were staring open-mouthed at Morning Glory Pool, and exclaiming "Ms. G., it's so cool!" It had finally hit them. Together we stand in awe at the top of waterfalls, sit on the steps of our cabins, and watch elk feed on the lawn. We laugh and get down and dirty in water fights. We bond. Somewhere along the line, we become a team.

After the Trip

We debrief and turn in field books in class the next day. We discuss our favorite parts, what we liked, what we didn't, and what we would do differently if we had it to do all over again. In the following weeks we collect photos for a giant wall collage. Student feedback is helpful to me for planning the next year. We usually take the trip the week before Memorial Day because it is approved by the school committee. It is an excused school absence, and there are no other assignments because English, history, and physical education are included in field-book assignments.

In Retrospect

Does it go well? Yes, beyond my wildest expectations. Is it without incident? No, but any incidents have been minor. The students want to show everyone they are mature enough to be trusted. Do they learn anything? For a while I wasn't sure, but in reading their field books I am always surprised. They put together the pieces we talk about all year long. Seeing it all in real life is the key to the big puzzle. The trip itself gives us a focus and a goal as a class. It is made clear from the beginning that only students I can trust are allowed to attend, so this virtually eliminates discipline problems in the classroom because students want me to be able to trust them.

However, the very best part is social. Students volunteer to carry backpacks for those who are tired or sore. Without a word from me, the group mothered a handicapped boy. They helped him with his field book, constantly retied his shoes, and invited him to dinner. Students who never associate at school hang out together. It is one big group the whole time. Students realize that the smart kids are pretty valuable when you are doing science all day, so no one is left out. Whenever I see any of them now, they are in the middle of a group.

Is it worth the hundreds of hours planning time? The uncountable gray hairs and antacids I consume? Yes, a million times. It is an event that epitomizes why we teach in the first place—to really connect with the students' lives and share with them the wonder of science. Students need out-of-class activities to make science more real. Once, as we were saying good-bye as parents picked up their tired, dirty, caffeine-overloaded children, a football player much bigger than I am swept me up in a bear hug and said, "Thanks Ms. G. It was the best time of my life. Thanks for believing in us. I love you." He walked away, and

I knew that no matter what else happened, that trip was a success. And, oh yes, we are already planning our next field-trip extravaganza.

Valarie Giacalone is an eighth-grade science teacher at North Cache 8/9 Center in Richmond, Utah.

Reference

National Research Council (NRC). 1996. *National Science Education Standards.* Washington, DC: National Academy Press.

The Wrap on Raptors

By John T. Tanecredi

I t was truly an exhilarating experience to help a flock of the American kestrel—a migrating hawk species—for the first time. It was exciting not only because we spent three hours attempting to attract North America's smallest hawk, but also because, once we captured this animal, placing the band on its leg allowed me to see this fabulous creature up close. So, it was no quantum leap in judgment when I shepherded a biology club day trip to Millington, New Jersey, for a hands-on experience with more than 1,100 birds of prey rehabilitated at the Raptor Trust, Inc.

Different Kinds of Raptors

A raptor is a bird of prey such as a hawk, eagle, falcon, or owl. Eagles, buzzards, falcons, kites, and condors are all diurnal birds of prey that belong to the order Falconiformes. Approximately 280 species of these birds exist. These predators have sharp, hooked beaks and powerful talons. Barn owls, screech owls, and snowy owls are examples of nocturnal birds of prey that belong to the order Strigiformes. There are approximately 140 species of owls, recognized by their heavy bodies, bulky heads, large eyes, neutral-colored plumage, silent flight, and acute hearing. Raptors are at the top of their food chain and are important in maintaining bio-

logical diversity. Owls, which eat mostly small mammals, are great rodent-control systems because they eat considerable numbers of mice and rats. The bones and fur of the prey are then regurgitated in an undigested pellet. Dissecting these dried pellets makes a great classroom exercise for students of any age; the bones can be removed from the pellet and reconstructed into a skeleton of the prey.

Rehabilitation

It has been estimated that tens of thousands of birds of prey are lost, injured, or otherwise prevented from migrating each year by untimely collisions with tall buildings, cars, trucks, and hunters. Len Soucey, director of the Raptor Trust, has rehabilitated thousands of birds and keeps several species in viewing cages. They are held in captivity because, due to their injuries, they cannot be released into the wild. Teachers and students can visit the Raptor Trust—either in person or via the internet—to observe the captive birds. Some species include the American bald eagle, the golden eagle, the goshawk, the red-tailed hawk, the peregrine falcon, the barn owl, the snowy owl, the long-eared and short-eared owls, and the American kestrel.

The Raptor Trust has a classroom facility that allows for workshops, lectures, or general question-and-answer sessions regarding raptors. The rehabilitation clinic houses a raptor hospital that conducts surgery and other rehabilitation therapies for the injured or sick birds brought to the professional curators. At The Raptor Trust, as well as other bird rehabilitation facilities, a cadre of dedicated veterinarians, teachers, students, and professors volunteers their time feeding newly born chicks, carefully administering bandages to wings of adult red-tailed hawks, or observing the eating behavior of short-eared owls brought into the hospital. If someone should come across an injured bird of prey within the New York metropolitan area, the Raptor Trust should be contacted for instructions on its care until either they come to get the bird or they tell you where to take it.

Protecting the Flock

To protect raptors and maintain their survival, one can help safeguard their habitats and breeding grounds. Protect the forest habitats! We should try to prevent pollutants such as oil, metals, and pesticides from getting into water or air, because these contaminants ultimately accumulate in small animals, which raptors eat, potentially passing their contamination to the birds. Pollution can alter their reproductive and developmental processes.

If you have the opportunity to bring your flock of students to an avian conservation facility similar to the Raptor Trust, your students' spirits will soar. You can arrange a visit by e-mail (*www.theraptortrust.org*). Can't get to the Great Swamp National Refuge in Millington, New Jersey? No problem! There are a number of raptor observatories throughout the country.

The Birds of Prey Foundation is a facility constructed on Boulder County Parks and Open Space land in Colorado. Although not open to the general public, this facility contains 227,300 cubic feet of flight space and is surrounded by 1,000 acres of farmland. Serving as a large outdoor hospital for raptors, the foundation that supports this land has looked after 151 golden eagles, 36 bald eagles, 34 peregrine falcons, and one Mexican spotted owlet. The website's virtual tour will take you to the facility's Intensive Care Unit (ICU) and Flight Enclosures.

The Raptor Research Foundation is a nonprofit scientific society. Their mission is to accumulate and disseminate scientific information about raptors (hawks, eagles, falcons, and owls), to inform the public about the role of raptors in nature, and to promote the conservation of raptors whose populations are threatened by human activities. The foundation's membership, which includes more than 1,200 individuals from more than 50 countries, consists of academic researchers, government employees, and laypersons interested in birds of prey. RRF was organized in 1966 and started publishing a scholarly journal titled *The Journal of Raptor Research* in 1967. In addition, the foundation holds annual meetings at which research on raptors is presented.

Thomas Cade, a professor of ornithology at Cornell University, founded The Peregrine Fund in 1970. The Peregrine Fund was created as a result of great concern over the possible extinction of the peregrine falcon. The members of the organization wanted to learn more about how falcons could breed in captivity. Their goal is to release the young into the wild to reestablish the peregrine falcon in the eastern United States and to increase peregrine populations in the western United States. The organization consolidated its facilities in Boise, Idaho, in 1984 and much has happened since then. The Peregrine Fund has not only propagated and released peregrine falcons into the wild, but also successfully released bald eagles, and helped save the mauritius kestrel from extinction.

The Golden Gate Raptor Observatory (GGRO) is run by three staff members and approximately 250 community volunteers with a common aim to study the autumn hawk migration. The observatory is open to the public. Members of the GGRO believe that public involvement is crucial in fostering long-term wildlife conservation. The GGRO's mission is to inspire the preservation of California raptor populations. The GGRO was formed in the early 1980s to track the Bay Area migration of thousands of raptors, including hawks, eagles, and falcons.

The Whitefish Point Bird Observatory near the National Wildlife Refuge in Whitefish Point, Michigan, is open to the public and records the chronology and volume of migrating bird populations through the Whitefish Peninsula Migration Corridor. Located on the northeastern tip of Michigan's Upper Peninsula, Whitefish Point serves as a haven for migrating raptors, water birds, and songbirds. The surrounding land and water features create a natural corridor for thousands of birds each spring and autumn as they travel through the Great Lakes region. This makes for spectacular bird-watching and provides tremendous opportunities to study and monitor bird populations.

Whether you are able to visit a raptor center or just experience one virtually through the internet, these centers are crucial for fostering a compassion for wildlife in distress and teaching new generations through mentorships, internships, lectures, and volunteer programs about the science of an essential species.

John T. Tanecredi is a professor of Earth and marine sciences at Dowling College in Oakdale, New York.

Internet
Bald eagle nest cam
   www.firstlightpower.com/eagles/default.asp
The Canadian Peregrine Foundation
   www.peregrine-foundation.ca
The Birds of Prey Foundation
   www.birds-of-prey.org
Golden Gate Raptor Observatory
   www.ggro.org
Hawk Migration Association of America
   www.hmana.org
Hawk Mountain Sanctuary
   www.hawkmountain.org

Welcome to the Congo

By Alison Ormsby

Imagine looking out your classroom window and seeing a wolf's monkey climbing up a strangler fig tree, a grey-cheeked hornbill looking back at you, or red river hogs rooting in the soil. What I've just described is a reality in the new Congo Gorilla Forest classroom, a unique learning environment at the Bronx Zoo.

Here, teachers participate in workshops that take them to exotic settings to observe the behavior of gelada baboons and much more. At the Bronx Zoo, it's easy to forget that you're in New York and not on a savanna or in a rain forest.

Each summer, middle school teachers from across the country attend a five-day training workshop to learn how informal science institutions, such as zoos, museums, nature centers, and parks, can expand the walls of their classrooms and stretch their students' inquiry into new areas. The Bronx Zoo's Education Department is particularly well-known for its active role in developing extensive curriculum programs that can be used in the classroom. In fact, each curriculum developed by the department includes activities that help teachers make the most of informal science institutions and transcend the typical field trip experience to create memorable learning events.

The Bronx Zoo's Diversity of Lifestyles curriculum shows teachers how to capitalize on students' inherent love of the animal kingdom. One year's workshop featured activities on the individual adaptations of land, air, and water animals. Curriculum activities, for use both in the classroom and at an informal science center, included animal locomotion, diet, habitat, climate, animal behavior, and human impact on wildlife. For example, in the activity Foot Notes, students completed an activity sheet in the classroom before going to an informal science institution in search of animals with different walking styles (see Figure 1). To prepare, students learned terms such as *plantigrade* (flat-footed), *digitigrade* (toe walkers), and *unguligrade* (nail walkers). In the African Plains exhibit at the Bronx Zoo, summer workshop participants could take a close look at plantigrade gelada baboons and unguligrade Nubian ibex.

Figure 1.
Foot notes.

INSTRUCTIONS: Check any and all categories below that apply to the animals you see at the zoo. One example is done for you.

ANIMAL	TYPE OF FOOT							TYPE OF TAIL		Habitat(s) (F = Forest) (G = Grassland) (D = Desert)	Where it lives (continent)	Notes on Movement
	Flat footed	Walks on toes	Hooved (on tip toe)	Digging Claws	Climbing Claws	Opposable toes	Hopping feet	Prehensile tail	Balancing tail			
Giant Armadillo	✓			✓						F, G	North and South America	Basic Gait (hard to see); rolls up in ball; shuffles

All of the curriculum materials offered by the Bronx Zoo meet the National Science Education Standards. For example, the Foot Notes activity mentioned above fits the life science standard for diversity and adaptations of organisms, structure, and function in living systems, as well as regulation and behavior. In addition to meeting the Standards, the Diversity of Lifestyles curriculum provides real-world connections. Students apply their critical-thinking skills to current conservation issues such as whaling and the wild bird trade.

The Diversity of Lifestyles curriculum is one of two modules in the program Wildlife Inquiry through Zoo Education (WIZE). Thousands of teachers in 46 states have been trained in the WIZE program. In addition, Diversity of Life-styles has been translated into Mandarin and is now used in four provinces of China. Both modules of the WIZE curriculum, Diversity of Lifestyles for grades 6–8 and Survival Strategies for grades 7–12, have been independently evaluated. The evaluators found that students participating in WIZE scored significantly higher on multiple-choice content tests covering life science concepts than students not exposed to the curriculum. In addition, teachers trained in WIZE reported a heightened awareness of the role that zoos can play in teaching science. What's more, nearly two-thirds of administrators surveyed perceived that teachers using WIZE were more enthusiastic about teaching science than they had been before taking the program.

Trained teachers have had very positive reactions to the Diversity of Lifestyles curriculum. David Allerheiligen, a teacher at St. John Lutheran School in Milwaukee, Wisconsin, says, "The program gives you the hook to catch the students' attention. Then it gives you the support, materials, and methods needed to cover the topic, maintaining student interest while increasing their knowledge and awareness. Students love the activity-based, high-participation format."

Note

For more information about the WIZE program or upcoming teacher workshops, visit the Wildlife Conservation Society at *www.wcs.org/education.*

Alison Ormsby is a teacher trainer in the Education Department of the Wildlife Conservation Society based at the Bronx Zoo in New York City, New York.

Hot Spot at Yellowstone

By Abby Dress

Yellowstone National Park is deservedly famous for the dynamic processes that occur below ground. Those processes are why a visit to Yellowstone National Park is not only a unique experience but also a really "cool" opportunity to observe hydrothermal features. From the north gate that leads visitors to the main interpretive center and the hot springs in Mammoth on down to where Old Faithful Geyser has been thrilling sightseers and scientists alike with its regular eruptions for years, visitors cannot help but notice the entire region seems like a steamy hot spot. In the truest sense, it is.

Within this huge national park (more than two million acres spread across Wyoming, Montana, and Idaho) are steaming geysers, hot springs, bubbling mudpots, and fumaroles, or steam vents. Drives on the main roads of Yellowstone take tourists through the major hot attractions, which also include Norris Geyser Basin, Upper and Lower Geyser Basin, West Thumb, and Mud Volcano. This unfenced territory, however, steams and smokes off the beaten track as well. That is because Yellowstone "preserves the largest hydrothermal area on the planet," says the official trail guide. Its hidden volcanic, tectonic,

and hydrothermal forces are constantly at work underground reshaping the landscape.

According to geothermal expert Henry Heasler, park geologist at the Yellowstone Center for Resources, Yellowstone has the largest concentration of active geysers in the world and more than 10,000 hydrothermal features. None of these would exist, however, without the tremendous hot rock, or geothermal source, beneath the surface.

The world's first and largest national park is a hot spot, which contains the Yellowstone Caldera. This is one of a few dozen such hot spots on Earth where heat from the Earth's interior is brought from the mantle closer to the surface. Some scientists theorize that the magma plume hovers within 13 km. Pressure from the molten rock is so close to the surface that it has created two bulges, or domed areas, at the park. One is located north of Yellowstone Lake and the other east of Old Faithful near Mallard Lake.

Believed by scientists to be about 640,000 years old, the Yellowstone Caldera is quite young geologically and is about 48 by 72 km in size. It originally was formed through subsequent volcanic eruptions that began in western Idaho and northern Nevada some 16 million years ago. Volcanic activity continues to this day in Yellowstone. Geologist Heasler says that hundreds to thousands of earthquakes occur there each year. It is a dynamic environment, in which even the ground constantly moves up and down, accruing changes of about 2.5 mm a year due to the massive volcanic energy.

Hot springs are the most common hydrothermal resources found in the park. Their activity constantly changes, particularly since these features are influenced by seasons and weather. Readily available sources of water from snow and rain trickle through the porous rock and are heated by the magma close to the surface. This superheated water circulates up and cools as it reaches the surface. Then it is replaced by hotter water from below and the cycle continues. This ongoing process is called convection. Hot springs typically do not reach the temperatures that lead to eruptions associated with geysers.

Windows Into Wonderland

A website designed for middle school students at *www. windowsintowonderland.org* is sponsored by the Yellowstone Park Foundation through Eyes on Yellowstone, which is made possible by Canon U.S.A., Inc. This free site features 50-minute electronic field trips that let students travel through the backcountry of Yellowstone National Park, the world's first and oldest national park, which remains one of the last wildernesses in the United States. Yellowstone, which is primarily situated in Wyoming, but also crosses into Montana and Idaho, has a greater number of a greater variety of free-roaming wild animals in their natural habitat than anywhere else in the 48 contiguous states.

Students can learn about the park's unique predator-prey relationships, geothermal activities, geological richness, and extraordinary wildlife. The trips feature scripted dialogue, animations, streaming video, and audio content. Lesson plan ideas, a vocabulary list, and appropriate links are included online to extend the experience.

Travertine is found in four thermal areas of the park, but the expansive travertine terraces found at Mammoth Hot Springs draw the most tourists. The whitish-gray terraced landscape looks like some scene expected on a visit to another planet. Limestone, or calcium carbonate, was deposited here millions of years ago when seawaters covered the area. When hot water from the springs is added to the rock, it dissolves the calcium carbonate. This carbonate is carried to the surface by the thermal waters and then left behind as travertine when they recede.

Microscopic bacteria and algae also thrive in many of the hot springs. These thermophiles thrive in water that is much too hot for most other life forms. These primitive organisms grow and are influenced by the temperature and chemistry of the hydrothermal pools. Some pool-wall edges are ringed with sequential color bands from these organisms. From the hotter-water areas on out to the cooler rims, these life forms are distinguished by color—yellow, green, red/orange, and brown, respectively. One specialized microbe, *Sulfolobus acidocaldarius*, feeds on sulfur compounds in the water. Oxidizing these, the organism turns the compound into sulfuric acid. Some pools become so acidic with a pH of 1.3 that they inhibit the growth of the more colorful bacteria and algae prevalent in most of the hot springs.

Visitors mostly come to see the geysers at Yellowstone. Geysers are also hot springs, but their plumbing is constricted. They not only depend on a water source for their eruptions but also create their own pressurized system. When underground, the hot water forms a pool or fills a fissure. Heated by the molten rock, the hot waters rise and coat the walls with silica, creating a tighter seal. Both the rock and water pressure ultimately prevent the water from cooling or vaporizing. Even though the water temperature increases and exceeds boiling, it remains in a liquid state. The result is superheated water that is less dense than the heavier water that sinks around it. As this superheated water rises, steam forms. The steam expands as it nears the surface.

Steam bubbles literally and forcefully push the water up and out of geysers. Cone geysers have more narrow jets of water, while fountain geysers spray water in different directions. During both these processes, steam and boiling water are expelled faster than cooler water can enter. Though pressure and heat begin to decrease during the expulsion process, the eruption stops when the water reservoir empties of hot water. There is an interval of time between eruptions that depends on the size of the water source and how close it is to the hot rocks.

Mudpots are hot springs turned into gurgling muddy pools that often have pungent odors. They tend to be acidic, unlike most of the park's hot springs and geysers. With their limited water supplies, steam is formed underground. This steam tends to break down the rocks chemically and clay forms. Over time, steam, hydrogen sulfide, carbon dioxide, and other gases burst through the clay as escaping bubbles. Minerals, such as *sinter* (a form of silica), sulphur, and iron, are responsible for the mudpot colors, gray, yellow, red/orange, and black, respectively.

The fumaroles or steam vents are the hottest hydrothermal features. Their limited water supplies are converted almost entirely into steam before escaping to the surface. From close up, these vents hiss loudly and spit out steam and gases. Large steaming plumes can be seen that make the hills look like they are smoking. On the one hand, these areas look like some cataclysmic aftereffect; on the other hand, the huffing and puffing activity makes the mountainsides look alive.

It should be noted that Lake Yellowstone, North America's largest high-altitude lake at about 2,500 meters above sea level, also has thermal activity. At its north end near Mary's Bay, scientists have discovered hydrothermal pits at the lake's bottom with temperatures above the boiling point. In other parts, where hot areas also have been recorded, spires made of diatoms about 30 m tall have been documented. Currently, no one seems to know how these towers were formed.

This is the magic of Yellowstone. It is a paradox of landscapes. From the forests of lodgepole pines that grow tall despite shallow roots and survive in the rocky soil of Yellowstone's Grand Canyon to the great plains of Hayden Valley, where one of the domes of molten rock is not so far below, Yellowstone National Park is a scientific treasure trove. It is a constant work in progress and a challenge to monitor, but one that provides exciting new discoveries and knowledge all the time.

Abby Dress is an associate professor of media arts at Long Island University's C.W. Post Campus in Brookville, New York, and works with Yellowstone National Park and the Yellowstone Park Foundation.

Resources

Smith, R., and L. J. Siegel. 2000. *Windows into the Earth: The geologic story of Yellowstone and Grand Teton National Parks.* New York: Oxford University Press.

U.S. Department of the Interior U.S. Geological Survey. 1995. *Yellowstone: Restless volcanic giant.* Volcano Hazards Fact Sheet. Open-file report 95-59, U.S. Geological Survey.

Yellowstone National Park. 2003. *Yellowstone resources and issues 2003.* Mammoth Hot Springs, WY: Division of Interpretation, National Park Service.

Index

*Page numbers in **boldface** type refer to figures.*